The Dreammakers Manual For Mortgage Lending!

An Instruction Manual for Making a Great Living in the Mortgage Business!

Wes Cordeau

authorHOUSE™

1663 LIBERTY DRIVE, SUITE 200
BLOOMINGTON, INDIANA 47403
(800) 839-8640
WWW.AUTHORHOUSE.COM

First published by AuthorHouse 09/12/05

ISBN: 1-4208-6482-3 (sc)

Printed in the United States of America
Bloomington, Indiana

This book is printed on acid-free paper.

Table of Contents

About The Author   vii

Dedication!   ix

Introduction   xi

    Who Makes The Best Loan Officer Candidates?   1

    The Psychology Of Lending!   10

    Completing An Application For Fun And Profit!   19

    Completing A Good Faith Estimate And TIL!   30

    Marketing!   37

    Flyers That Work   57

    BY REFERRAL ONLY   69

    DataBase Mining!   85

    Wholesale Lenders Are Your Friends!   97

    Websites That Work!   103

    Funny Stories   110

    "Cordeauisms"   117

    The Final Thoughts!   127

    Glossary Of Mortgage Terms   129

    Appendix   143

Onward we go, learning more how to be a highly paid professional mortgage loan officer!

If you have an interest in joining this dynamic team, call 281-445-1901, X204 for the "President's Hotline"
or
Email: Wes@TexasSupremeMortgage.com

About The Author

Wes Cordeau is the Mortgage Broker, and President of Texas Supreme Mortgage, Inc. (TSMI) in Houston Texas. His clients embellished him with the moniker:

"The Dreammaker"

soon after he became involved in the direct lending business.

He became "The Dreammaker", because he makes the "dreams of the borrowers" come true at closing through homeownership!

He is an active producing mortgage loan originator while managing Texas Supreme Mortgage. He has been in the direct lending business since February, 1989, and started Texas Supreme Mortgage in July, 1993. Mr. Cordeau has also been a licensed Texas Real Estate Broker since 1980. Prior to being actively involved in the mortgage business, Mr. Cordeau was in the property management business and obtained the highest level of accreditation, The Certified Property Manager status, for a period of ten years. His background in accounting, real estate and property management is perfect for being a professional mortgage loan officer.

Texas Supreme Mortgage is one of the largest mortgage broker production offices in Houston, and Texas with many loan officers active in loan production.

Texas Supreme Mortgage's website is: www.TexasSupremeMortgage.com

They are continually searching for quality loan officers to join their team. Their training programs set the industry standard, and any new or experienced loan officer can earn a substantial income while learning the mortgage business and maximizing their potential.
Many of the loan officers were referred by account reps to TSMI.

The only thing holding any loan officer back at Texas Supreme Mortgage is their own desire and drive, because the tools set in place can be used to excel to the next level!

If you have an interest in joining this dynamic team, call 281-445-1901, X204 for the "President's Hotline"
or
Email: Wes@TexasSupremeMortgage.com

Dedication!

This book is dedicated to my lovely wife of many years, Molly Sue, or as I must call her now, "Dr. Molly", since she has recently obtained her Ed.D in the field of education. She has been a silent supporter of my dreams, convictions and confidence for over 30 years.

Without her, life would be incomplete!

Our children, Brian and Brad have endured the gentle onslaught of my ideas and thoughts, for their entire life. Many of my ideas were formed and presented to our children as my "focus group", prior to being used in the field.

Brian's wife, Kristi recently joined our family and is now a "willing" participant in this great scheme of learning! Little did she know of this until after we "tricked" her into marrying into the family! She is a welcome addition to our family and we are happy to have her boundless enthusiasm!

Without my wife and these three children, life would be incomplete!

This book is also dedicated to the many people I've met throughout my life that have made an impact on me. Some have made a huge impact, while others were just a fleeting moment of time, but none the less impacting.

My theory is that our life is like a great quilt. This quilt starts developing the moment of our conception and will continue until the last moment prior to our passing. Every person we have encountered, and some we haven't personally encountered have a patch on our great quilt.

Obviously, some people will have a giant patch and others just a tiny patch on our quilt.

Two ex employers that have made a huge positive impact on my quilt were Jim Hunt in Houston, and John Bushman in Odessa Texas. Both of these men showed me what real integrity looked like in the business world. Mr. Hunt and Mr. Bushman were the shrewdest, smartest and humblest businessmen I've met, and they showed by their actions that you could do well financially while not compromising your principles or integrity. Even though it was many years ago that I worked for these men, their impact is still with me daily. Both taught me to make long-term decisions, not decisions based on today's needs! Even today, if there is a question, I'll think, "What would Jim or John do in this situation?" Once I see the answer as they would, the decision is easy!

Another individual that has been of paramount importance in my life is Joe Stumpf, of California, Founder and National Spokesperson of the BY REFERRRAL ONLY organization. I have learned from Joe to think on a higher plane than ever before. Joe's ability to succinctly summarize phrases and put them into practical usage has been extremely important to me in my personal development. I have watched in awe of Joe's ability to bring out the best in people he works with in the BY REFERRAL ONLY seminars. I have also learned that it's "progress, not perfection" when approaching business and personal development.

I can only hope that I could be as impacting on one person in my life as Jim Hunt, John Bushman and Joe Stumpf have been in mine!

Introduction

Why this Book?
Why Now?
What does this book offer that hundreds of others don't?

The origins of this book were back in 1964, when Wes was playing Little League baseball for the Groves Realty Little League team (you remember; the orange team) in Groves Texas! Groves is a small town in Southeast Texas sandwiched between Port Arthur, Orange and Beaumont, in what is known as the Golden Triangle. This is oilfield country! Most of the employment was in the many major refineries, and most young boys aspirations were to work in one of the "good paying" oil refinery jobs starting right after high school and continuing until retirement or death, whichever came first.

When the All-Star Little League baseball season was over in late July, Wes went to Mr. Booth, an "elderly" white haired gentleman of 50 or so that owned Groves Realty, and asked Mr. Booth if he could sell real estate for him prior to school starting. Even at 12 years old, Wes knew he would be involved in some facet of real estate for his livelihood. Unfortunately, he had to wait a few years to become involved—and he did!

He knew he would never work in an oil refinery.

This book offers the reader an inside look at the mortgage business from a marketing and general knowledge standpoint. This book is written so that the beginning mortgage originator just starting their career can excel. The knowledge gleaned from this book will propel the beginning originator to into the ranks of the surviving originators, instead of being cast away as so many in the past have been cast aside! Once they learn to survive in this business, then they can thrive.

This book is also written so that an experienced loan originator can pick up pointers for marketing strategies and ideas that they have never thought of before, or encapsulated in the method presented. The experienced originator will be able to gain insight from a marketing genius through reading, adopting and adapting the strategies in this book.

This book also has enough positive influences within the covers to fulfill an entire book standing alone. Reading this book offers a game plan for marketing and production, and hope for the future. The psychological approach to lending has never been discussed as it is in this book. This book is written with enthusiasm, which has been one of the leading hallmarks for Wes during his entire life.

Integrity, Enthusiasm and constant Learning combine to form the foundation for all his successes.

This book is written in a first person account by a highly experienced, "hands-on" loan originator at the core. Wes Cordeau has written this book from the heart, and is right on target when it comes to working with people in a very detailed and delicate transaction. The mortgage process is one of the most tedious of all projects that most families ever undertake. Few families would put themselves through the torment of the mortgage process, except to obtain the ultimate prize—The American Dream, Their Own Home!

This book will teach the novice and highly experienced loan originator how to have a life, and a work life too! The reader will not want to skip or skim over any portion of this book because on every page is some pearl of wisdom, both concerning the mortgage business, and living a fulfilled and fun filled life!

The lively accounts of Funny Stories and "Cordeauisms" add immensely to the overall enjoyment of the entire book. Each story does have a subliminal message attached to it.

Ultimately, this book is destined to become a classic on mortgage marketing, and quite possibly a classic on marketing in general!

Enjoy reading this book as much as Wes enjoyed writing it.

Onward we go, learning more how to be a highly paid professional mortgage loan officer!

If you have an interest in joining this dynamic team, call 281-445-1901, X204 for the "President's Hotline"
or
Email: Wes@TexasSupremeMortgage.com

Who Makes The Best Loan Officer Candidates?

Over the last 100 years, I'm quite certain that there have been exhaustive studies on loan officers and the best qualities of each one. We certainly have our standards, but one attribute stands out over all the rest that I have noticed for success:

The, "I Will" Is More Important Than The "IQ"!

If you will simply follow directions of those leaders you trust, and work daily, you can make a good living in this business. I have seen high school dropouts make it, and highly educated college grads with advanced degrees NOT make it, simply because they failed to follow the basic steps of marketing and progression.

Some of the characteristics we look for are in the following flyers that have helped us secure the right type of person as a loan officer. These are great recruiting tools.

What Is A 5 Star Loan Officer?

A **5 Star Loan Officer** meets the following criteria:

1)   They Are Open For Ongoing Dialogue; They will talk to you.

2)   They Are Friendly; Someone we would want to work with.

3)   They Are Willing To Make A Decision In The Next 1-3 Months.

4)   They Know What They Want In A Career And In Life.

5)   They Would Like You To Help Them In Their Career.

If we spend our time working with 5 Star Loan Officers, we will have a successful organization. These are the people we will be most successful serving, and therefore they will also be the ones who refer to us the most loan officers just like themselves!

Remember, Birds Of A Feather, Flock Together!

You will notice that a 5 Star Loan Officer is not built upon education or past experiences. They just need to meet the criteria listed above and have a burning desire to succeed!

This flyer is designed to let potential loan officers know and understand what TSMI expects and their behavior on a long term basis for current and future individual growth.
We find that this list is a guide for successful loan officers to follow.

Are You A Low Maintenance Person?

At Texas Supreme Mortgage, we are looking for a few select Loan Officers to complete our cadre of producing Loan Officers. We are looking for a few Low Maintenance individuals that can meet the criteria set below. We find that the individuals that can meet the criteria set below thrive in our system. Those that do not meet the standards do not do well in our system, and we feel it is better for all parties that they choose other employment.

1) **Do you have the ability and desire to tell the truth?**

2) **Do you feel compelled to be 100% responsible for your actions and activities?**

3) **Do you feel a deep responsibility to keep all of your commitments?**

4) **Do you understand the importance of being on time for commitments?**

5) **Would you recommend yourself with enthusiasm?**

6) **Are your actions and integrity referable?**

7) **When a transaction is completed, would clients talk to you, or about you?**

8) **Do you exude a high level of trust so your clients rely on you for your expertise and integrity?**

9) **Do your clients know how much you care about them and their situation?**

10) **Once the transaction is complete, would you keep in contact with your clients on a recurring repetitive basis?**

11) **Do you have the ability to appreciate additional input into your efforts?**

This list, while detailed is in no way complete as to the overall attitude required at Texas Supreme Mortgage, Inc. We expect that your client will be respected beyond their expectations and in return we expect their loyalty to TSMI.

This flyer is designed to give the benefits to loan officers for working at TSMI! Every relationship has a "give and take" component. This is the "give" portion from TSMI!
The "5 Star Loan Officer" and "Low Maintenance Person" flyers earlier addresses the "give" portion from the potential loan officers!

Who Is The Next Person That

1)   Wants to make a change, because they are **Dissatisfied** in their current position?

2)   Wants to **Increase** their Income Dramatically?

3)   Wants to Learn More about the **Mortgage Business** from an Industry Expert?

4)   Wants to Learn More about **Marketing**?
In fact become an **Expert** in Marketing?

5)   Wants to Learn How to Build a Mortgage Business, **and** have a **Life** Too?

6)   Wants to Learn How to Build a Mortgage Business on a **Referral Only** basis?

7)   Wants to Learn How to make a **Six Figure Real Income**, ALL Thru Referrals?

8)   Wants to Learn How to Have a solid Business and take **30 days Vacation** too?

9)   Wants to Work for the man, **"Who Wrote The Book On Mortgages"**?

10)   Wants to Learn the Mortgage Business from an **Entrepreneurial Millionaire**?

Do any of these criteria meet your current situation, needs or desires?

If you or someone you know that has the desire to better their life, please have them contact the following representative of Texas Supreme Mortgage for an appointment:

Wes Cordeau, "The Dreammaker"
281-445-1901, x204
Email: Wes@TexasSupremeMortgage.com

Can You Really Make A Fantastic Living In This Business?

All over the country, there are many people making a prosperous income as a mortgage loan officer. The methods employed may be as diverse as the people employed in the business and as diverse as their borrowers. The economics of lending are pretty simple from a mortgage brokerage company standpoint:

Gross Income:
The mortgage brokerage receives its income from various sources: Origination Fees, Yield Spread Premiums, Service Release Premiums, Processing Fees and assorted "junk fees"! These junk fees will have various names associated with the fees. Just remember they all end up in the coffers of the mortgage brokerage.

HINT: There are NO FREE loans, even though some big name companies advertise, "No Cost Loans", believe me these loans are not FREE, or no cost. There is always a cost associated with a mortgage loan, either rate or fees. Alas, that is another entire book on the subversive methods some of the national lenders use to "hook" the unsuspecting borrowers. You want to work with a local mortgage broker that you trust!

Expenses:
The mortgage brokerage expenses are similar to most service businesses. The staff payroll, rent, marketing, office supplies, and assorted other expenses are all fairly standard within the industry. The largest expense would usually be the loan origination splits to the loan officers.

The mortgage brokerage business is not a capital intensive business, which is great for a low cost entry and potentially high return. However, this same ease of entry is also what drives the competition into the business when the pickings look easy for this "low hanging fruit!" It is this same ease of entry that drives the "fly by niters" to the business when rates are low, and refinances are plentiful.

This ease of entry is also the attribute that drives the builders, realtors, insurance agents and a host of other service people to become mortgage brokers as an additional source of income to their main business of building, real estate or insurance. I can't necessarily fault them for trying; however customer service usually suffers when the crossovers occur, rather than helping the consumer and lowering their overall cost of lending. Any time you have a profession as a sideline, the consumer does not get the best service. They may get acceptable service, but not extraordinary service. Training is usually woefully inadequate at best. Again, you can't fault them for trying to pick up some extra revenue; however the consumer needs to beware of this type of organization.

Loan Officer Expense:
Now, back to the original question:

Can You Really Make A Fantastic Living In This Business?

Absolutely you can make a fantastic income as a mortgage loan officer. I can testify to that, however, before we go to the pie in the sky numbers, let's see what some of the real life numbers look like:

- 50% of all people licensed will not make a penny in the business
- 25% of all people licensed will close two transactions or less and leave the business
- 15% of all people licensed will **make a living** in the business
- 8% of all people licensed will make a **prosperous income** in the business
- 2% of all people licensed will make a **fantastic income** in the business

Still with me, still want to quit your $60,000 a year steady pay accounting job to pick up the easy income and freedom by being a mortgage loan originator?

Let me define those numbers above:

- The 15% making a living are in the $40-60,000 annual average income
- The 8% making a prosperous income are in the $80-120,000 annual average income
- The 2% would be in excess of $150,000 annual average income

These statistics are what I like to call **"Cordeau Stats",** meaning they may or may not be statistically correct but, based on my knowledge of the industry would be as accurate as any high priced government monitoring system or study!   These statistics are more of a SWAG, rather than a **WAG!** If these are new terms to you, SWAG is a Scientific Wild Assed Guess, whereas a WAG is simply a Wild Assed Guess!

If you read this book, I can guarantee you one thing; you will have the tools and knowledge to make a fantastic living in this business. What you do with those tools would be simply up to you, and your "I WILL" or otherwise known as drive, desire and ambition!   What motivates you to success?

Ok, let's look at more real life numbers! In order to make a fantastic income, ALL you have to close is 4-8 transactions monthly, and you are there. It's not magic! Let's assume you close six transactions monthly, and the average loan size is $200,000. In many parts of the country that is a low loan amount and in some parts that is a high loan.

A reasonably average commission for Origination and Yield Spread Premiums would be in the 2-3% range. A FNMA loan would most likely be 2% whereas a sub-prime loan would be at 3% total fees to be distributed.

> **WARNING: There are no standard fees set for any type of loan. These are merely estimates based on my personal industry experience. The commission earned from the borrowers is highly negotiable, and can range from almost 0-7.99% before it becomes a high-cost loan! Do You Hear Me Now!**

If you are generating your own clients, a 60% split is easily attainable. To survive in this business you must learn how to generate your own clients. Use your selling skills to enhance this split with your knowledge from reading this book and any industry experience and other training that is available to you.

CALCULATION: Loan Amount   X   Fees   X   LO Split % = Transaction Income
$200,000   X   3%   X   60%   = $3,600 P/Transaction

Close 6 Units Monthly X $3,600 P/ Transaction =
$21,600 monthly, $259,200 Annual Fantastic Income!

Ok, let's say you aren't that good of a negotiator, or can't ask for the business, and only receive 2% commission on these six units monthly:
6 Units X $200,000 Loan Amount X 2% Fees X 60% Split X 12 Months =
Only $172,800 Annual Fantastic Income for 6 units monthly!

These are not smoke and mirror numbers! In a lower cost area like Houston for instance, the loan amount may be lower, say $140,000 average, but the overall commission would be closer to 3%, so the income is still fantastic!

CALCULATION: Loan Amount X   Fees   X Split   X 12 Months   =
$140,000   X   3%   X 60%   X 12 Months   =
Only $181,440 Annual Fantastic Income for 6 units monthly!

Obviously, there are as many variations on income combinations and splits as you could explore forever. Just know that by closing 6 units monthly, a mortgage loan officer can make a **fantastic income**. So why do only 2% actually make this fantastic income? What happens to the other 98% along the way to the money fountain?

We'll look at that phenomenon a little later!

OK, you don't believe me concerning wages of the normal loan officers! Below and on the next page are listed the government statistic on wages for loan officers! You know this has to be accurate!

Even the US Department of Labor says that in the 90th percentile, the loan officers are earning $82,640 in 2000! So it is easy to see that after five years of home and loan appreciation and a little effort, the numbers and percentages listed above in my SWAG should be fairly accurate.

2000 National Occupational Employment and Wage Estimates

13-2072 Loan Officers (Government Definition)

Evaluate, authorize, or recommend approval of commercial, real estate, or credit loans. Advise borrowers on financial status and methods of payments. Include mortgage loan officers and agents, collection analysts, loan servicing officers, and loan underwriters.

These estimates are calculated with data collected from employers in all industry divisions in metropolitan and non-metropolitan areas in every State and the District of Columbia.

Employment estimate and mean wage estimates for this occupation:

Employment	203,530	RSE = 2.2 %
Mean hourly wage	$22.96	RSE = 1.1 %
Mean annual wage	$47,760	RSE = 1.1 %

Percentile wage estimates for this occupation:

Percentile	10%	25%	50% (Median)	75%	90%
Hourly Wage	$11.64	$14.72	$19.92	$27.52	$39.73
Annual Wage	$24,200	$30,610	$41,420	$57,250	$82,640

What percentile will you be in? With just a little effort, you can be in the fantastic percentile!

OK, back again! Why do people give up on their dreams of earning a fantastic income and slink back to their old jobs or try the next HOT THING without really giving this business their total effort? I dunno! Really, I can't figure it out. The numbers don't lie. The income potential is there, but it does take some effort and skills.

The skill set is pretty deep for success in this industry. Although the skills required are numerous, there are no skills that are hard to obtain. The basic skill set I like to see is:
- Integrity
- Desire to succeed
- Ability to think on your feet
- Desire to succeed
- Some math abilities
- Desire to succeed
- Ability to present ideas to one or more people
- Desire to succeed
- Ability to explain documentation required
- Desire to succeed
- Ability to communicate effectively
- Desire to succeed
- Ability to follow up on details
- Desire to succeed
- Ability to ask for the business

- Desire to succeed
- Ability to risk rejection, and overcome any short term rejection
- Desire to succeed

There are probably another 50 skill sets that are good for this business. However, if you have Integrity and a Desire to Succeed you will flourish in this business. The mortgage lending business is just not that hard. On the other hand, it's not simple either; otherwise the industry would hire minimum wage clerks to get the job completed.

The business is out there for those willing to take the steps to insure their short term and long term success in this business.

When you decide to or decided to join this industry, you may have thought it was a temporary fix to an immediate financial problem. However, if you treat the business as a profession, and not a "Mortgage Thing", you will do well. Too many people think of this business as a stopgap measure to something else. If you treat it as long-term business, this can be a fantastic profession for the long haul. However, it is not a "Mortgage Thing". Have you ever asked your CPA if he was still doing that "CPA Thing" or your Cousin the Doctor if she is still doing that "Doctor Thing"? No, because these professions are treated and act as professionals in their daily routine, and we need to do the same.

This form on Planning and Accountability was devised to help the LO in their overall planning. Monthly, I have an "Hour of Power", where we will discuss a specific marketing or business idea in detail. This form has proven to be most helpful for the new and experienced Loan Officer in getting a handle on their goals and follow up!

Not all of the information included for our "Hour of Power" is included here.

Planning And Accountability

Planning
1) Are you involved in any daily planning now?
2) Need a balance between personal and business.
3) Review this weeks planning and progress.
4) Systematic approach.
5) Tools and aids to planning.
   - ABC Guide
   - Two Week Planner
   - Daily/Monthly Planner
   - Annual Vacation Planner
   - Article On Planning
6) Action Cures Fear

Accountability

1) What are your fears concerning being accountable?
2) Who are you accountable to?
3) Why do we need accountability, or do we really need it?

4) What will you be accountable for in the next: Week _____
_____
_____
_____
Month_____
_____
_____
Year_____
_____

5) When do you want your **Accountability Partner** to call you **weekly** to discuss your weekly progress?

Name: _____ Cell:_____

Day_____ Time _____AM PM
(Circle One)

Can You Really Make A Fantastic Living In this Business?

(HINT: It's Up To You!)

Onward we go, learning more how to be a highly paid professional mortgage loan officer!

**If you have an interest in joining this dynamic team, call 281-445-1901, X204 for the "President's Hotline"
or
Email: Wes@TexasSupremeMortgage.com**

The Psychology Of Lending!

Loan Applications

In each lending transaction, there are a myriad of players and participants. All of them can get in your way to getting a loan closed, and generally when ANYTHING goes wrong, they will all point to the Loan Officer (LO), and the mortgage company for blame! Many of the players receive their remuneration from the transaction, regardless of a successful closing.

Studies have shown that the borrowers are at one of the top three stressors in their life when obtaining a mortgage; 1) Death of a close family member, 2) Divorce, 3) Obtaining a Mortgage. Sometimes, all three stressors are in play during the same transaction.

It is our job to smooth out the wrinkles and ruffled feathers of all the players. Each borrower must be made to feel that they are the only transaction you have in process right now. No borrower wants to know, nor do they care how busy you are.

Remember, ALL people listen to that famous radio station;

WIFM: What's In It For Me!

Even the best of borrowers are looking out for their own self interest. Now, there's nothing inherently wrong with that, we just have to deal with it and the other player's interest also, and finalize the transaction in a timely manner!

The loan officer has a dual capacity to the client and to the loan process. We must be a technician to determine that the loan will meet certain lending guidelines, yet we must also be a cheerleader of sorts to spur on the client in the decision making process. Even before the client ever is introduced to us, we must be great in marketing to the real estate agents or other referring sources. So ultimately, we will wear many hats during the transaction. It would be similar to the copier salesman coming back out to repair or service the machine during the warranty period. In that realm, different people serve the separate functions of marketing and repair, however, not in the mortgage business. The loan officer wears both those hats.

The LO's primary job at application is to tell the borrowers the truth, the whole truth, and nothing but the truth, so help you God! Sounds simple enough, right? In reality, many LO's will tell the borrower anything the borrower wants to hear. The LO feels certain if they tell the borrower the whole truth, then the borrower will leave to another mortgage company!

It should be absolute policy for the Loan Officer to under promise and then overdeliver to the client!

I once had a LO that would tell the borrower anything they wanted at application. If an application clearly indicated it was a Sub-Prime borrower, this LO would still quote them a FNMA rate and term, knowing full well that was wrong. (FNMA rate is short for Federal

National Mortgage Association, and along with her "brother" company, FHLMC, Federal Home Loan Mortgage Corporation controls the conforming mortgage market)

His theory was that later, when we received the loan approval, he would "sell" the client on the terms of the actual approval. If we are performing our job right, and for the long-term, we should be considered consultants, not salesmen.

Consultants do things FOR the clients!
Sales people do things TO the clients!

Sadly, this loan officer was able to "sell" the new terms to the clients on several occasions before I found out what was happening. His statement was "don't worry, the loans will still close, and were all getting paid"! On each loan, even if it did close, the borrower would NEVER refer anyone, because they felt like they were "baited and switched" right before closing! Truth is, that's exactly the result.

This LO ultimately had a nervous breakdown, and then a year later went to work for another local mortgage company. Later, over 25 people were convicted of mortgage fraud in a mortgage flipping scheme at his new employer. Several served time in federal prison for their fraud. I was thankful; he only worked for me a few months under tight supervision before leaving under duress!

Back to the Borrowers!

These same borrowers, if told the truth at application, would have understood they were not FNMA borrowers, because they knew their credit had severe problems. However, when the "professional mortgage" LO tells them at application, "No Problem, this rate and term should be OK", the borrowers begin to believe they are a better credit risk than what is truthful. During the course of the transaction, they keep hearing from the LO, "everything's on track", the borrower is even more sure they are now, "God's gift to the mortgage company"! Not realizing, it's all about to blow up as soon as the underwriter looks at the file for approval!

So what if the borrower, "can't handle the truth" (like Jack Nicholson in "A Few Good Men"), then let them go to the next mortgage company and waste their time. The best thing that can happen with an unreasonable client is to blow them out at application. Save your time, energy and effort for those clients that appreciate what you do for them.
If you "coddle" the borrower at application, you will have a big problem throughout the mortgage loan process.

One of my favorite sayings is "Take the Bull by the Horns". If you do this at application, the problems during the transaction are minimal. Most clients want someone to lead them through the transaction, because lending is like a foreign language to most "normal" people! Since many LO's are not considered "normal" anyway, we completely understand the language of lending.

Loan Application Tasks

The loan application should accomplish several important tasks:

- Ascertaining the seriousness of the borrower in this transaction
- Completing a formal application
- Completing a Good Faith Estimate to determine estimated payment and total cash required for this transaction
- Determining the most appropriate mortgage loan for the borrower
- Completing a Qualification Worksheet to determine ability to borrow
- Obtaining a complete list of source documents from the borrower
- Building a rapport so that they understand and trust us
- Describing the mortgage lending process so they understand what is involved
- Describe the method by which we obtain our clients, via "Referrals"
- Introduce them to the staff—a behind the scenes look at the company
- Finalize any additional documentation that is remaining

My personal loan applications are usually a lot of fun. I don't try to rush them through the application process. This is the time to build rapport with the borrowers face to face.
I get to know them, and find out what's important about buying a home and this home specifically. I also tell them about my family, and some of my background.

When the application is completed, you would think we are old friends. Don't most people like to trust their largest financial decision with an old friend? Yes, of course.
Over the years, I've had many people open up at application more than they would to a high priced Psychologist!

I've heard some LOs brag, "I can get a loan application completed in 20 minutes".
Too bad I think. Usually we only see a borrower at application, and again at closing, or celebration, as some people call it. These are the two times we can display our depth of knowledge, compassion and trust. We are there at both times when the borrower most needs us and our expertise.

Many borrowers will come to us at application scared to shivers! I've literally seen people shaking with fear at application. If you see this, take the time to settle them down, and listen to what fears they have surrounding the mortgage process! People come to us in all stages of life. Some will come just after a divorce, and they have never bought anything by themselves before. Maybe their ex-husband always took care of the financial details and this is the first and giant step in their new life. Spend a few extra minutes with them explaining the process, and showing them how they qualify for the mortgage on their own now! Think of the application process this way: How would you want your elderly grandmother treated? Then treat each person the same way!

Some people will come into the application process worried that they can't buy a home because of past and current credit issues, cash requirements or income issues. I have a wall with a board full of pictures of borrowers at closings. I point out to the applicants that 80% of all the people on the board had at least one area that was a problem, cash, credit or income.

They are all smiling happy homeowners now. This picture of success in the application or conference room is very important.

Remember, what we can visualize, we can accomplish. If the borrowers see other families that went ahead of them in the process and are now happy homeowners, it will alleviate some fears.

Fun Stuff At Loan Application

It is not the huge dramatic things we do for a borrower and their family that stands out to them later, but the many simple little things we do that makes a difference in the overall experience with you as a mortgage professional. Many lenders will have a board in the lobby welcoming the "Smith" family to the mortgage company. They may have a welcome packet available to each family. We have already discussed some of the aspects of the application, but here are some specific things we do for a borrower, why, and the results.

Refreshments!

When a borrower enters our lobby, the receptionist acknowledges them by name, and offers them a soda, coffee or bottled water. This lets them know we are expecting them and respect them enough to acknowledge them by name! The receptionist then notifies the LO that the "Smiths" have arrived for their 2PM appointment. The LO comes to the lobby welcomes them with open arms, introduces himself, and asks if they have met "Linda", the receptionist. He then tells the borrower that Linda is the lovely voice they will hear many times during the transaction. They then proceed to the conference room.

Music!

We try to have music playing in the background in our application room that the borrowers like. If you can figure out what type of music they like, play it "softly" in the background. If you can't figure it out, ask them before they come in what is their favorite type of music or artist. Then have that music playing. Music that we are familiar with puts us at ease, and makes us comfortable even in an uncomfortable situation! We want the borrowers to feel comfortable during the application process!

Sometimes it is just not convenient to have the specific type of music playing; in those rare instances we play Baroque classical music. I don't know anything about classical music, but I read that Baroque classical music was soothing to people. It seems to work, and the CD's are inexpensive!

We actually have a stereo system in our application room and another in my office a couple of doors down. If I have an applicant on Saturday or in the evening, we can "crank up" my high powered system and have a little fun. Because of this idea, and using CD's as a reward system for myself, I now have a collection of over 300 CD's.

I've bought several CD's specifically because the borrower told me they like "Kenny G" or "Boney James" as their favorite artist for instance! Some have been used once, but most have been a welcome addition to my collection.

Toys For The Kids!

If the borrower has children at the application, I always make a point to shake hands or high-five the children, and make them feel just as welcome as the parents! In the conference room, we have a basketful of small toys for boys and girls. I will tell the children that if they are really good at the application, they can pick out a toy to bring home with them to keep forever. Usually at this time, I'll ask the children "Are you going to be real, real good for us so we can get you and your parents a new home?

Of course they always nod or say YES! I'll "almost" always agree that I know they are going to be real good and quite, so go ahead and take the toy now before we get started.

As you already know, if someone treats your child with care and consideration, you as a parent feel wonderful towards the person giving the care and consideration.

In eight years, I've only had one set of children that didn't get a toy, although not all were saintly perfect! I have many children that will accompany their parents back when bringing additional documents so they can get another soda and a toy. Sometimes they will ask if they can bring a toy home to another brother or sister that is not at the application. **DON'T BE STINGY WITH THE KIDS TOYS!**

Think about it! The cost of the toy is $1.00 at the dollar store, and a 25 cent soda, we make friends for life because the experience was a little better than expected.

Pictures!

Another thing we do at application is take a picture of the family or individual. Actually, I take three pictures, or have three copies made. I've had two different digital cameras, and ended up frustrated with the output, and gave these to my sons for their use. It was probably an operator malfunction! I use my 35MM camera and it works just fine!

I send one picture each to the family and to the Realtor with a little note that proclaims, "The Smith Family" at application. The third picture is next to my processors desk so that she knows who we are working for. We have been known to include a picture in the submission package to the lender, so they can see who we are working for in this transaction. Many times for the children, I'll have them "pose" separately and include their pictures with the family pictures. If this sounds a little corny, it may be, but it's all part of the process to make the family and their children feel comfortable with the overall experience.

Trinkets!

We also have trinkets like pens and notepads that we send them home with so they remember us forever and ever, and tell their friends about the application process!

Make the application process fun, informative and productive for everyone and this is the beginning of a successful mortgage transaction and relationship.

We also have a list of the next steps concerning the transaction, and what we need and expect from the borrowers before closing. I put this list on bright pink paper so the borrowers can remember where to look for information. This list is in the Appendix., as Instructions to Clients!

The Hierarchy of "Love" In A Mortgage Transaction!

In every mortgage transaction, the relationship starts off as if everything will be perfect. Shortly after the application, the "Love" starts to diminish until Approval is obtained. Once approval is certain, the "Love" again rises **almost** to the level it was at application.

This is why it is of utmost importance to get as much of the initial information at the first meeting. Even, if this meeting has to be delayed, it is better to start the application, and ultimately loan processing with a full set of documents. This detail will keep you from going back to the borrower several times for additional information. The borrower will forget that they were the one who did not initially bring the initial source documents, and only remember that they seemed to be harassed by the lender in obtaining more information.

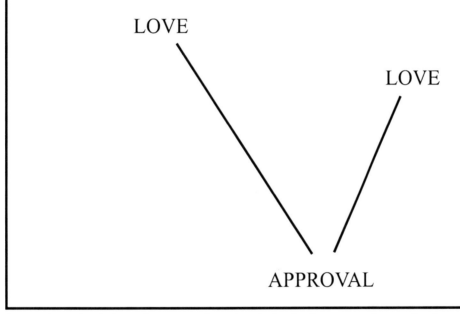

LOVE

LOVE

APPROVAL

Several methods have been employed to help the borrower know the importance of bringing all the source documents to the initial application. I have given $20 gift certificates to a local restaurant, two movie tickets and "gold stars", like when we were kids in elementary school!

If you are giving the gift certificate and/or movie passes, be sure the client knows what to bring to application, and the expectation of receiving the gift for having all of their documentation at the initial application. Tell them up front, if you bring all of the items requested, there will be a huge reward for your efforts at the application. People will work very hard for a $20 gift certificate. In reality, if they know the importance of the source documents up front, they will usually make every attempt to bring the information. In practice, if the borrowers made a good effort to bring everything, and maybe left off one or two items—give them the certificates, with the promise of getting you the remaining item by the next day or two.

The most cost effective reward is the "gold stars". Remember when you were a kid in elementary school. The teacher would give you a gold star for a "neat" paper or for a 100 on a spelling test. This is the same principle. Give the client a Gold Star for bringing all their source documents! Ahh—Heck—Give em two or three, and their kids too!
You laugh, but people would prance around the office with these gold stars like they were a million bucks!

Really, what were doing is appealing to people's base instinct for recognition!

How motivated is the borrower sitting in front of you?

This meter I've developed may help you recognize where the borrowers are in their home buying process. Fax the meter to them and have them complete it before arrival.

This form is used to qualify and quantify the borrowers desire to purchase a home in the near future, or to include them on a "tickler" file for in the future. Hopefully, most of your clients are at the 8-9-10 motivation level. The money level is the 8-9-10 levels; however your database may be filled with borrowers from all levels to develop a pipeline of leads for future business.

Keep all contacts on a database, or "tickler" file so that you can follow up with them by email, snail mail and/or phone. Constant communication with your database will payoff handsomely for years to come. It is the difference between being a mediocre performer and a long-term successful mortgage professional with a fantastic income.

Homebuyer Motivation Meter

Where are you at on the
Homebuyer Motivation Meter?

LOW: (1) I want to buy a home someday!

MED: (5) I want to buy a home in the next three to six months!

HIGH: (10) HELP!! I have a home picked out now or have a
burning desire to buy in the next 30 days!

Homeownership has many benefits. By working together, you
and your family can be a homeowner like many of our past clients.

Working with buyers in the 8-9-10 range will help us to meet our current income goals. However, clients in all numerical ranges are required to keep our pipeline full.

On the next page is a very important schedule; "The Continuum Of Lending"!

Every borrower is on an emotional roller coaster during the process of finding a home and obtaining a mortgage. The borrowers will almost always work their way thru the entire continuum between application and closing.

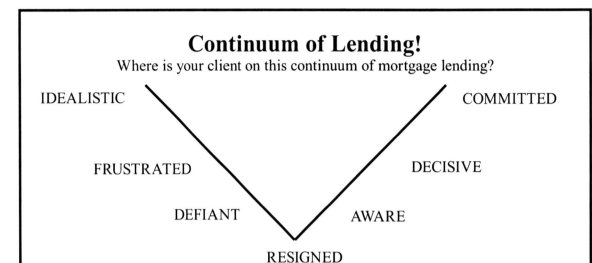

Continuum of Lending!

Where is your client on this continuum of mortgage lending?

DEFINITIONS:

Idealistic:	Everything will be perfect in this transaction!
Frustrated:	You mean you need more information!
Defiant:	No, I don't see why you really need this additional information!
Resigned:	OK, I'll give you the information, if I must for the loan!
Aware:	Now, I see how all the information ties together!
Decisive:	We will get the loan!
Committed:	Whatever it takes, let's close the loan and get the home!

Every individual or family will go thru and survive the various stages of the mortgage process. Unless it is a transferred file, every family will start off in Idealistic, and continue straight thru to Committed!

When we work together, this process is much more pleasant.

If you think about it, getting a mortgage loan is similar to courting! Almost every relationship starts off in the **Idealistic** mode, however before progressing to marriage in the **Committed** mode; there are times when the couple will be in any and all of the other modes from **Frustrated** to **Decisive!**

Onward we go, learning more how to be a highly paid professional mortgage loan officer!

If you have an interest in joining this dynamic team, call 281-445-1901, X204 for the "President's Hotline"
or
Email: Wes@TexasSupremeMortgage.com

Completing An Application For Fun And Profit!

Purpose: To complete the loan application to include the 1003 and all associated documents so that the processor has a complete understanding of the file and source documents. A complete application will save time and energy in the short and long term.

Procedures: 1003 Section I; Terms of Loan, P.1

Only if the loan is ready to be locked will this section be completed at initial application. The estimated information for rate, term and amounts will go on the GFE (Discussed Separately).

Uniform Residential Loan Application

This application is designed to be completed by the applicant(s) with the Lender's assistance. Applicants should complete this form as "Borrower" or "Co-Borrower", as applicable. Co-Borrower information must also be provided (and the appropriate box checked) when ☐ the income or assets of a person other than the "Borrower" (including the Borrower's spouse) will be used as a basis for loan qualification or ☐ the income or assets of the Borrower's spouse will not be used as a basis for loan qualification, but his or her liabilities must be considered because the Borrower resides in a community property state, the security property is located in a community property state, or the Borrower is relying on other property located in a community property state as a basis for repayment of the loan.

I. TYPE OF MORTGAGE AND TERMS OF LOAN					
Mortgage Applied for: ☐ VA ☐ FHA	☐ Conventional ☐ USDA/Rural Housing Service	☐ Other (explain):	Agency Case Number		Lender Case Number
Amount $	Interest Rate %	No. of Months	Amortization Type:	☐ Fixed Rate ☐ GPM	☐ Other (explain): ☐ ARM (type):

If the borrower has a home or is refinancing will you complete this section at application.

1003, Section II; Property Information and Purpose, P.1

Subject Property: Only if there is already a property chosen, or on a refinance will this information be completed at the initial application. Get the ***legal description*** from the old title policy or contract. Most are lot and block descriptions. On a refinance, complete the line on ***when purchased*** and all details. I usually put some amount in for a "General Remodel". Be sure to ask the applicant how much has been spent for any upgrades or improvements. Estimate a number, say $5,000!! The information on ***title names*** is very important. The name they put here will be signed 42 times at closing. So, if they use the seven names of their prior husbands, all seven have to be signed on each form. Also, watch out for any suffixes such as Jr., Sr., III, etc. Nicknames, like "Buddy", or "Bubba" is not acceptable.

Manner in which title is held is usually "jointly", or "joint tenants" or "solely", for married and single individuals. "Jointly", will usually be used to indicate a married couple. "Joint Tenants", will usually be used for an unmarried "couple" buying a home. "Solely", is used for a single person. *Estate* will almost always be Fee Simple in Texas. We almost never do a loan on a lease hold. *Source of Down Payment* needs to be documented and traced, also known as "source and seasoned" by the underwriters!

II. PROPERTY INFORMATION AND PURPOSE OF LOAN		
Subject Property Address (street, city, state, ZIP)		No. of Units
Legal Description of Subject Property (attach description if necessary)		Year Built

Purpose of Loan ☐ Purchase ☐ Construction ☐ Other (explain): ☐ Refinance ☐ Construction-Permanent

Property will be: ☐ Primary Residence ☐ Secondary Residence ☐ Investment

Complete this line if construction or construction-permanent loan.

Year Lot Acquired	Original Cost $	Amount Existing Liens $	(a) Present Value of Lot $	(b) Cost of Improvements $	Total (a+b) $

Complete this line if this is a refinance loan.

Year Acquired	Original Cost $	Amount Existing Liens $	Purpose of Refinance	Describe Improvements ☐ made ☐ to be made Cost: $

Title will be held in what Name(s)	Manner in which Title will be held	Estate will be held in: ☐ Fee Simple ☐ Leasehold (show expiration date)
Source of Down Payment, Settlement Charges and/or Subordinate Financing (explain)		

1003, Section III; Borrower Information, P.1

Again, use suffixes, but not nicknames. Most information here is self-explanatory. *Years in School*--just estimate, say 16 for college grad, 14 for some college and 12 for HS. *Children*, use only children living in the household that are 18 and younger. Over 18 are considered independent, even though they may not be. *Present and prior addresses*-most people can't remember how long they have lived at the current address and prior. If they say 12 months at the current and 12 at the prior residence or apartment, you better go ahead and get the third address too just to be safe. Better to get it verified and not need it, rather than scramble at the end to get the 22-24th month verified. Remember, the "Love" is highest at application!

This is on rental verifications; mortgage information is usually on the credit report. If not, do a direct Verification of Mortgage (VOM). I would suggest getting their Cell #'s, and ask who is the best person and time to contact them if a question arises.

Borrower	III. BORROWER INFORMATION	Co-Borrower
Borrower's Name (include Jr. or Sr. if applicable)		Co-Borrower's Name (include Jr. or Sr. if applicable)

Social Security Number	Home Phone (incl. area code)	DOB (MM/DD/YYYY)	Yrs. School	Social Security Number	Home Phone (incl. area code)	DOB (MM/DD/YYYY)	Yrs. School

☐ Married ☐ Separated	☐ Unmarried (include single, divorced, widowed)	Dependents (not listed by Co-Borrower) no. ages	☐ Married ☐ Separated	☐ Unmarried (include single, divorced, widowed)	Dependents (not listed by Borrower) no. ages

Present Address (street, city, state, ZIP) ☐ Own ☐ Rent ___ No. Yrs.	Present Address (street, city, state, ZIP) ☐ Own ☐ Rent ___ No. Yrs.
Mailing Address, if different from Present Address	Mailing Address, if different from Present Address

If residing at present address for less than two years, complete the following:

Former Address (street, city, state, ZIP) ☐ Own ☐ Rent ___ No. Yrs.	Former Address (street, city, state, ZIP) ☐ Own ☐ Rent ___ No. Yrs.

1003, Section IV; Employment, P. 1

Name/Address of Employer-usually from the W-2, but make sure that the address listed is the address that will be verifying employment. Verify at least two years of employment. If in doubt get 3 years to be sure. Some people will have one job, and I've seen one with 6

jobs in two years. **Yrs on the job** are really with this employer. **Yrs employed in field,** is the estimated total time in the field and related jobs.

   Position/Type of Business is a broad-based description, i.e.; clerk/retail, attorney/service. Be sure to get any *extensions* for their phone systems. Also, get the direct phone number to *Human Resources* so that the processor may contact them directly if required.

Borrower			IV. EMPLOYMENT INFORMATION		Co-Borrower	
Name & Address of Employer	☐ Self Employed	Yrs. on this job	Name & Address of Employer	☐ Self Employed		Yrs. on this job
		Yrs. employed in this line of work/profession				Yrs. employed in this line of work/profession
Position/Title/Type of Business		Business Phone (incl. area code)	Position/Title/Type of Business			Business Phone (incl. area code)

If employed in current position for less than two years or if currently employed in more than one position, complete the following:

Name & Address of Employer	☐ Self Employed	Dates (from-to)	Name & Address of Employer	☐ Self Employed		Dates (from-to)
		Monthly Income $				Monthly Income $
Position/Title/Type of Business		Business Phone (incl. area code)	Position/Title/Type of Business			Business Phone (incl. area code)
Name & Address of Employer	☐ Self Employed	Dates (from-to)	Name & Address of Employer	☐ Self Employed		Dates (from-to)
		Monthly Income $				Monthly Income $
Position/Title/Type of Business		Business Phone (incl. area code)	Position/Title/Type of Business			Business Phone (incl. area code)

Freddie Mac Form 65   01/04
Calyx Form 1003 Loanapp1.frm 01/04

Page 1 of 4

Borrower _____
Co-Borrower _____

Fannie Mae Form 1003   01/04

1003, Section V; Income and Housing Expense, P.2
Processing Standards to use: This formula must be committed to memory!

Weeks in one year: 52   Months in one year: 12
Work Weeks in one Month: 52wks/12mo = 4.33 Work Weeks in One Month
Hours in Work Month: 40 hrs/week X 4.33 = 173.33 hours in work month
Weekly Employee: Paid weekly
Semi-Monthly Employee: Paid twice monthly, usually 15th and last day of the month
Bi-Weekly Employee: Paid every other week, say, every other Friday
Monthly Employee: Paid once monthly-usually seen in government payrolls
Bi-Monthly Employee: One that would be paid every other month (seldom used)

So computing **base wages** on an hourly employee is 173.33 X $12/hour = $2,079.96, say $2,080.monthly. Of course, a semi-monthly base wage would be 2 times their base gross wages per paycheck.

Overtime, Commissions, Dividends/Interest-Must be able to verify in existence for 24 months and then average. In reality, after about 18 months some lenders will allow the use of additional income.

Net Rental Income-Use the base rental income times 75%, LESS any mortgage payment. i.e., $1,000 rent X .75 =$750 (usable), less mortgage (PITI) of $695 = $55 NET Income for our purposes!!

Other Income-This is for DOCUMENTED child support, social security, pensions, etc. This must be documented to be in existence for 12 months, and continuing for 2-3 years. Child support that is paid thru a state or county agency can be easily verified. If paid privately, get 12 months cancelled checks. If in existence under 12 months, get all documentation on payments made, and a reasonable letter of explanation.

IF a borrower has more than 25% of their income from commission or overtime, **OR ANY** rental income and it is a full doc loan, you must include last two years tax returns. **Not necessary on stated income!! (You would be surprised how many new loan officers, and some experienced ones will include a tax return on a "stated income" loan!)**

V. MONTHLY INCOME AND COMBINED HOUSING EXPENSE INFORMATION						
Gross Monthly Income	Borrower	Co-Borrower	Total	Combined Monthly Housing Expense	Present	Proposed
Base Empl. Income*	$	$	$	Rent	$	
Overtime				First Mortgage (P&I)		$
Bonuses				Other Financing (P&I)		
Commissions				Hazard Insurance		
Dividends/Interest				Real Estate Taxes		
Net Rental Income				Mortgage Insurance		
Other (before completing, see the notice in "describe other income," below)				Homeowner Assn. Dues		
				Other:		
Total	$	$	$	Total	$	$

* Self Employed Borrower(s) may be required to provide additional documentation such as tax returns and financial statements.

Describe Other Income   *Notice:* Alimony, child support, or separate maintenance income need not be revealed if the Borrower (B) or Co-Borrower (C) does not choose to have it considered for repaying this loan.

B/C		Monthly Amount
		$

In the Appendix is a handy Qualification Worksheet that can be used. We require it to be completed prior to a file being processed. If the loan officer can't figure out how the borrower will be qualified and approved, how can the processor proceed with the file?

1003, Section VI; Assets and Liabilities, P.2

    Assets-*Cash deposit* on a purchase, money held by the title company, builder or seller.

    Bank Accounts-Use the latest statement balance on each account needed. Get ALL pages of each account. Complete the address section for your processor. She should have it in an auto input, but maybe not.

    Stocks/Bonds/IRAs--Same, all pages and paper trail of large deposits

Note any large deposits, and document where the deposit came from with a paper trail. Lenders are very careful when large deposits are made to determine and document that they are not illegal funds routing through the accounts. The Federal penalty for illegal money used for the down payment can be confiscation of the home, and canceling of the entire mortgage!! It is of extreme importance to properly account for the source of any large bank deposits, and sourcing of recent funds into the bank accounts!

Real Estate Owned--This is a summary from p.3 of the 1003.

Life Insurance, net Cash Value-Use only if substantial and you can document cash value.

Businesses Owned--Estimate value based on a current balance sheet. In reality, very seldom used.

Auto—and other toys, like motorcycles, boats, etc. Try to determine value based on some reasonable valuation, but also try to have the value at least equal to the note payoff.

Other Assets--Estimate of household goods, anywhere from $25k to $250K. $40-75,000 is an estimate I use on a purchase up to $250, 000.

Always check if completed jointly or not.

Wes Cordeau

VI. ASSETS AND LIABILITIES

This Statement and any applicable supporting schedules may be completed jointly by both married and unmarried Co-borrowers if their assets and liabilities are sufficiently joined so that the Statement can be meaningfully and fairly presented on a combined basis; otherwise, separate Statements and Schedules are required. If the Co-Borrower section was completed about a spouse, this Statement and supporting schedules must be completed about that spouse also.

Completed ☐ Jointly ☐ Not Jointly

ASSETS Description	Cash or Market Value	Liabilities and Pledged Assets. List the creditor's name, address and account number for all outstanding debts, including automobile loans, revolving charge accounts, real estate loans, alimony, child support, stock pledges, etc. Use continuation sheet, if necessary. Indicate by (*) those liabilities which will be satisfied upon sale of real estate owned or upon refinancing of the subject property.		
Cash deposit toward purchase held by:	$			
		LIABILITIES	Monthly Payment & Months Left to Pay	Unpaid Balance
List checking and savings accounts below		Name and address of Company	$ Payment/Months	$
Name and address of Bank, S&L, or Credit Union				
		Acct. no.		
Acct. no.	$	Name and address of Company	$ Payment/Months	$
Name and address of Bank, S&L, or Credit Union				
		Acct. no.		
Acct. no.	$	Name and address of Company	$ Payment/Months	$
Name and address of Bank, S&L, or Credit Union				
		Acct. no.		
Acct. no.	$	Name and address of Company	$ Payment/Months	$
Name and address of Bank, S&L, or Credit Union				
		Acct. no.		
Acct. no.	$	Name and address of Company	$ Payment/Months	$
Stocks & Bonds (Company name/ number & description)	$			
		Acct. no.		
		Name and address of Company	$ Payment/Months	$
Life insurance net cash value	$			
Face amount: $				
Subtotal Liquid Assets	$			
Real estate owned (enter market value from schedule of real estate owned)	$	Acct. no.		
		Name and address of Company	$ Payment/Months	$
Vested interest in retirement fund	$			
Net worth of business(es) owned (attach financial statement)	$			
Automobiles owned (make and year)	$	Acct. no.		
		Alimony/Child Support/Separate Maintenance Payments Owed to:	$	
Other Assets (itemize)	$	Job Related Expense (child care, union dues, etc.)	$	
		Total Monthly Payments	$	
Total Assets a.	$	Net Worth **=>** (a minus b)	$	**Total Liabilities b.** $

Freddie Mac Form 65 01/04
Calyx Form 1003 Loanapp2.frm 01/04

Page 2 of 4

Borrower _____
Co-Borrower _____

Fannie Mae Form 1003 01/04

24

VI. ASSETS AND LIABILITIES (cont.)							
Schedule of Real Estate Owned (if additional properties are owned, use continuation sheet)							
Property Address (enter S if sold, PS if pending sale or R if rental being held for income)	Type of Property	Present Market Value	Amount of Mortgages & Liens	Gross Rental Income	Mortgage Payments	Insurance, Maintenance, Taxes & Misc.	Net Rental Income
		$	$	$	$	$	$
Totals		$	$	$	$	$	$

List any additional names under which credit has previously been received and indicate appropriate creditor name(s) and account number(s):

Alternate Name	Creditor Name	Account Number

Liabilities—Derived from the credit report, review with borrower, and list. I do not include addresses here, just the name and **current balance** from the credit report, unless we can document and update the credit report. Only go to that effort if the actual balance is significantly different from reported.

Alimony/Child Support--list who payable to and the monthly amount.

Job Related Expenses, if significant; however childcare is NOT considered an expense in Conventional lending.

Assets and Liabilities (cont), P.3

Schedule of Real Estate--self explanatory, but watch if a sale is anticipated, but not pending on the current homestead. If you mark it as "P", the underwriter will approve the file with it being a condition of being sold and closed. If it is listed for sale, but no sale pending, leave this block blank! Unless you are prepared to delay closing until the sale is consummated, the buyers will need to take the home off the market (or not list it to begin with), and get a lease on the current homestead. Otherwise, with no lease, you have to count both the new and old payment against the borrowers.

The problems with this line in the real estate section can be significant, and only occurs or is determined to be a problem at the very end of the transaction. Remember, this is when the "Love" is already at its lowest in the entire transaction.

1003, Section VII, Details of Transaction, P.3

On the initial application, this section should mirror the GFE. As a practical matter, this section is usually left blank on the initial hand written application since the GFE has the same numbers and information.

VII. DETAILS OF TRANSACTION	
a. Purchase price	$
b. Alterations, improvements, repairs	
c. Land (if acquired separately)	
d. Refinance (incl. debts to be paid off)	
e. Estimated prepaid items	
f. Estimated closing costs	
g. PMI, MIP, Funding Fee	
h. Discount (if Borrower will pay)	
i. Total costs (add items a through h)	
j. Subordinate financing	
k. Borrower's closing costs paid by Seller	
l. Other Credits(explain)	
m. Loan amount (exclude PMI, MIP, Funding Fee financed)	
n. PMI, MIP, Funding Fee financed	
o. Loan amount (add m & n)	
p. Cash from/to Borrower (subtract j, k, l & o from i)	

1003, Section VIII, Declarations, P.3

This is where you ask them if they have had any bankruptcies, child support, lawsuits pending, federal loans defaulted, foreclosures or any outstanding judgments. Also, you ask if they are a US citizen, or have a Green Card, and if they have been a homeowner before. **Read and understand this section!!**

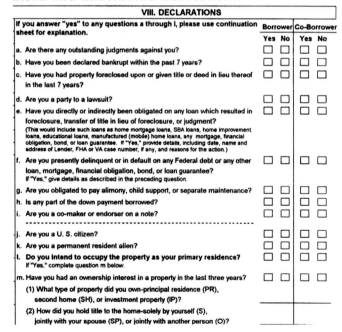

26

1003, Section IX, Acknowledgement and Agreement, P.3

In this section, they are stating and verifying that they are telling the whole truth, and nothing but the truth, so help them God! They need to sign and date here.

Read and understand this section!

IX. ACKNOWLEDGMENT AND AGREEMENT

Each of the undersigned specifically represents to Lender and to Lender's actual or potential agents, brokers, processors, attorneys, insurers, servicers, successors and assigns and agrees and acknowledges that: (1) the information provided in this application is true and correct as of the date set forth opposite my signature and that any intentional or negligent misrepresentation of this information contained in this application may result in civil liability, including monetary damages, to any person who may suffer any loss due to reliance upon any misrepresentation that I have made on this application, and/or in criminal penalties including, but not limited to, fine or imprisonment or both under the provisions of Title 18, United States Code, Sec. 1001, et seq.; (2) the loan requested pursuant to this application (the "Loan") will be secured by a mortgage or deed of trust on the property described herein; (3) the property will not be used for any illegal or prohibited purpose or use; (4) all statements made in this application are made for the purpose of obtaining a residential mortgage loan; (5) the property will be occupied as indicated herein; (6) any owner or servicer of the Loan may verify or reverify any information contained in the application from any source named in this application, and Lender, its successors or assigns may retain the original and/or an electronic record of this application, even if the Loan is not approved; (7) the Lender and its agents, brokers, insurers, servicers, successors and assigns may continuously rely on the information contained in the application, and I am obligated to amend and/or supplement the information provided in this application if any of the material facts that I have represented herein should change prior to closing of the Loan; (8) in the event that my payments on the Loan become delinquent, the owner or servicer of the Loan may, in addition to any other rights and remedies that it may have relating to such delinquency, report my name and account information to one or more consumer credit reporting agencies; (9) ownership of the Loan and/or administration of the Loan account may be transferred with such notice as may be required by law; (10) neither Lender nor its agents, brokers, insurers, servicers, successors or assigns has made any representation or warranty, express or implied, to me regarding the property or the condition or value of the property; and (11) my transmission of this application as an "electronic record" containing my "electronic signature," as those terms are defined in applicable federal and/or state laws (excluding audio and video recordings), or my facsimile transmission of this application containing a facsimile of my signature, shall be as effective, enforceable and valid as if a paper version of this application were delivered containing my original written signature.

Borrower's Signature	Date	Co-Borrower's Signature	Date
X		X	

1003, Section X, Government Monitoring, P.3

Even if the borrower does not want to furnish this information, we have to complete the information on Ethnicity, Race and Gender. In 15 years, I've only had one person that refused to give the information--just complete it, and if you don't know what nationality they are, ask!!

X. INFORMATION FOR GOVERNMENT MONITORING PURPOSES

The following information is requested by the Federal Government for certain types of loans related to a dwelling in order to monitor the lender's compliance with equal credit opportunity, fair housing and home mortgage disclosure laws. You are not required to furnish this information, but are encouraged to do so. The law provides that a Lender may discriminate neither on the basis of this information, nor on whether you choose to furnish it. If you furnish the information, please provide both ethnicity and race. For race, you may check more than one designation. If you do not furnish ethnicity, race, or sex, under Federal regulations, this lender is required to note the information on the basis of visual observation or surname. If you do not wish to furnish the information, please check the box below. (Lender must review the above material to assure that the disclosures satisfy all requirements to which the lender is subject under applicable state law for the particular type of loan applied for.)

BORROWER ☐ I do not wish to furnish this information			CO-BORROWER ☐ I do not wish to furnish this information		
Ethnicity: ☐ Hispanic or Latino	☐ Not Hispanic or Latino		**Ethnicity:** ☐ Hispanic or Latino	☐ Not Hispanic or Latino	
Race: ☐ American Indian or Alaska Native	☐ Asian	☐ Black or African American	**Race:** ☐ American Indian or Alaska Native	☐ Asian	☐ Black or African American
☐ Native Hawaiian or Other Pacific Islander	☐ White		☐ Native Hawaiian or Other Pacific Islander	☐ White	
Sex: ☐ Female	☐ Male		**Sex:** ☐ Female	☐ Male	

To be Completed by Interviewer This application was taken by:	Interviewer's Name (print or type)		Name and Address of Interviewer's Employer
☐ Face-to-face interview ☐ Mail ☐ Telephone ☐ Internet	Interviewer's Signature	Date	TEXAS SUPREME MORTGAGE INC. 505 N. SAM HOUSTON PKWY. E. STE.110 HOUSTON, TX 77060 (P) 281-445-1901 (F) 281-445-8805
	Interviewer's Phone Number (incl. area code)		

Freddie Mac Form 65 01/04		Fannie Mae Form 1003 01/04
Calyx Form 1003 Loanapp3.frm 01/04	Page 3 of 4	

Then the interviewer completes and signs the final block as to how the application was taken, and the broker's information.

1003, P.4 Continuation Page for additional Assets and Liabilities (Not Included here)

Completing Other Forms
All forms to be signed and dated by each borrower.
(Examples Are Included In The Appendix)

Borrowers Statement Regarding Active Duty Military: Declaring that they are, or, or not in a military reserve unit. The purpose of this for is to document the status of their outstanding potential reserve obligations. Under the 1940, Soldiers and Sailors Civil Relief Act (SSCRA), the lender may be prohibited from charging interest in excess of 6% per annum, while the reservist is on active duty, plus an additional six months upon returning from active duty. This act was revised and renamed The Service Members Civil Relief Act (SCRA) of 2003, in 2003. If we fail to document this potential event, the Mortgage Broker may expose themselves to liability from the lender. Let's look at an example. You close Mr. Smith on his new $200,000 loan, without this form, and his rate of interest on the 2/28 sub-prime loan is 8%. Shortly thereafter, his reserve unit is called up to active duty. The lender upon the request of Mr. Smith is obligated to lower his rate to 6%. The 2% Yield Differential the lender is losing may come from your pocket, if the reserve status is not properly documented. It is better to be safe than sorry later. (This form is not in the loan processing software)

Borrowers Certification and Authorization: Borrower is signing off as to the property being used as their homestead or investment property.
Have them write their SS # at the bottom.

Notice To Applicants: Borrower is stating that the SS# they wrote on the Certification is true and correct. Yes-they are an individual--so circle YES!

Transfer of Loan Servicing Disclosure: This form informs the borrower that the broker transfers 100% of our loans, since we do no loan servicing within the company. We are a mortgage broker (and proud of it too)!

Notice of Right to Receive a Copy of Your Appraisal; ECOA-B: This informs the borrower that they may get a copy of their appraisal.

Notice to Applicant; ECOA: This form informs the borrower that we will not discriminate against them based on race, color, religion, national origin, sex, martial status, age (w/ restrictions),..... Basically, if they have green money, we will work with them.

Good Faith Estimate Attachment: List of third party service providers and contact information.

Privacy Policy Notice: This informs the borrower that we collect "nonpublic personal" information, BUT do not share it with anyone except on a need to know basis. We do not sell their information to third parties.

Additional Disclosure For Fixed Rate Loans: This gives some of the basics of the loan as we know it at application, or an estimate. Also discloses that we are a broker and are charging fees for our services. (This form is not in the loan processing software)

Mortgage Broker/Loan Officer Disclosure: This form lists the LO's license # and how much money is being received at application, and how the funds will be applied, and if any is refundable. As a practical matter, if we collect for the appraisal, and do not spend the money, we will return the appraisal money to the borrower, less any third party fees, if the transaction fails to close and fund.

Credit Score Notice: This is a new form as of December, 2004, and mandatory as of February 1st, 2005. It comes from the FACT Act (Fair and Accurate Credit Transaction Act). This form is used to inform the client that they will be receiving a credit report with their FICO scores detailed. Have both borrowers sign on a joint report. If, two or more unmarried individuals are purchasing together, then a separate form for each borrower is required.

Good Faith Estimate: This form is a financial synopsis of the transaction. This form is discussed in detail separately.

Once the application and all associated forms are properly completed, the application is now ready to be sent to or turned in to the processor. However, before the file is turned in to processing several things have to be completed. A complete file includes the following information to processing:

1) **Completed Qualification Worksheet**: This form shows the processor and yourself that you should have a workable file within ratio parameters. If you, as the professional LO can't figure out how to make the file work, how will your processor?

2) **Communication Log**: This sets the overall tone for the file when turning the documents to processing. On this form, you would tell the processor which title company to use, appraiser, etc and any details that may not be on the application. For instance, you might tell the processor that the wife is the best contact rather than the husband. You might use this for cell phone numbers, or to tell the process that the husband only answers to "Bubba", instead of Elmer as listed on his application. This log is very important for the file from inception to closure.

Onward we go, learning more how to be a highly paid professional mortgage loan officer!

If you have an interest in joining this dynamic team, call 281-445-1901, X204 for the "President's Hotline"
or
Email: Wes@TexasSupremeMortgage.com

Completing A Good Faith Estimate And TIL!

Good Faith Estimate:
See Appendix For a Computer Example

Purpose: The GFE should reflect the best estimate of **cash to close** and **monthly payment** at time of application. This estimate is a compilation of many Lender's fees, and some may be higher or lower on an individual basis.

Completion: The LO should complete, explain, have signed by borrowers and the LO to sign at time of loan application. *USE WHOLE DOLLARS ONLY!!*

This document must be signed, faxed or delivered to borrowers within 3 business days of completion of the loan application. No Exceptions. If mailing the document, keep a copy for your records, and make a note of the date mailed to borrower.
I recommend completing or having the document completed at application.

The following description uses the Handwritten GFE as the basis for discussion. The theory is that if you can complete a GFE by hand, then you can complete it thru the computer.

There are six sections to the GFE that I use when completing by hand. Each loan processing system has a similar format for completing on the computer. The processor will use your input to complete the computer generated forms. The computer forms are used for the TIL, which is sent out by the processor within 3 days of signing the GFE and application. If the information substantially changes upon finding a home, then complete and have a new GFE signed for the updated information.

Section 1; Information
Self explanatory for **names** and **property address** if known.
Interest rate: The best estimate at time of application. Unless the loan is being locked today, put a small "e', with a circle around it to indicate "estimate"
Term: Use anticipated term, usually 30 or 15 years.
Type of Financing: Check which type is anticipated. Most loans will be CONV. Most sub-prime loans will be CONV/ARMS, "A" loans many times are Fixed. So in this area, there will be two checks-one on the top line, and one on the bottom.

☆*TEXAS*
SUPREME MORTGAGE, INC.

BORROWER _____ CO-BORROWER _____

PROPERTY STREET ADDRESS _____

INTEREST RATE _____ TERM _____ TYPE OF FINANCING ARM ___ FIXED ___ OTHER ___

CONV ___ FHA ___ VA ___

(**NOTE:** In this area just, it is best to put any terms that are anticipated. On sub-prime, it may be noted; *2 yr PPP, 2/28,* indicating that the loan is fixed for 2 years, then starts to adjust, and has a 2 year pre-payment penalty).

Section 2; Monthly Housing Expense
PI: Calculate on your financial calculator.
Other Financing: This would be for any second liens from the seller or third party.
Hazard Insurance: Monthly estimate of property insurance. This is **property insurance** covering fire, windstorm and hail damage. We do not require contents or replacement coverage. Most lenders will limit the deductible to no more than 1% of the value.
Real Estate Taxes: Monthly estimate.

MONTHLY HOUSING EXPENSE

First Mortgage (P&I)	$ _____
Other Financing (P&I)	$ _____
Hazard Insurance	_____
Real Estate Taxes	_____
Mortgage Insurance	_____
Homeowner Assn Dues	_____
Other	$ _____
Total Monthly Pmt	$ _____

Mortgage Insurance: Most "A" loans above 80% LTV will have mortgage insurance. You can **download** the expense chart from Radian, GE or other private mortgage insurance companies. (An 80-20, 80-10-10 or 80-15-5 loan will eliminate PMI)
This insurance is **default insurance** for the benefit of the lender, so our client does not have to make a 20% down payment. There is NO MI on Sub-Prime loans.
Homeowner Assn Dues (HOA): This is the neighborhood association fee. Even though most associations collect this fee directly from the homeowner, we must use it for our calculation of Debt To Income (DTI).
Other: Usually used for Flood Insurance.
Total Monthly Pmt: Total of other items above.

Section 3; Details Of Purchase/Refinance
Purchase Price: Actual from contract or anticipated sales price. Client will look to you as the professional for advice on maximum price they should pay based on their income and expenses, and comfort level of total debt.
Debt Payoff-Refinance: Use this line on Refinances. Get the information from their latest mortgage statement, compare it to the credit report, and update if needed when the actual payoff comes from the lender. If a discrepancy to the credit report--the latest statement is usually the most accurate. (30 days accrued interest will be added to the payoff in the prepaids section below Section 5)

DETAILS OF PURCHASE/REFINANCE

Purchase Price	$ _____
Debt Payoff-Refinance	$ _____
Total Closing Costs (Est)	$ _____
Prepaid Escrows(Est)	_____
Total	_____
Amount This Mortgage	(_____)
Other Equity/Financing	(_____)
Amount of Cash Deposit	(_____)
Closing Costs Paid by Seller	(_____) ****
Cash Reqd. for Closing	$ _____
Payment Cushion	$ _____
Total Assets Required	$ _____

Total Closing Costs (e): Compiled and explained in Section 4 below. (C/C)

Prepaid Escrow (e): Compiled and explained in Section 5 below. (P/P's)

Total: This is a subtotal of the purchase price, C/C and P/P's before any credits or mortgage is applied.

Amount This Mortgage: This is the anticipated amount of the first mortgage loan amount that we are obtaining for the borrowers.

Other Equity Financing: This is any second lien, either from the seller or third party. We may or may not be providing this mortgage, but need to account for its existence.

Amount of Cash Deposit: This is the amount of deposits ACTUALLY PAID for earnest money, appraisal, credit report and application fees (if any) at time of application. On a prequal, client may only have the credit report fees paid to us. This is NOT the down payment for the purchase.

Closing Costs Paid By Seller: Either per the contract, or anticipated, or required based on the borrower's cash availability. This must be **communicated** to the client and their Realtor, so that the contract is written to reflect the cash requirements from the GFE!

Note whether we are anticipating 3% or 6%, or some other % from the seller in the space provided. I usually "circle" the 3 or 6, and handwrite any other %'s required.

Cash Required for Closing: This is the "net" number from the calculation above.

Payment Cushion: Some lenders will require a payment cushion of one to two months of PITI. **Discuss this with your client.** If there is a shortage of funds, a gift may be obtained for this amount. The lender, if required, does not keep this cushion, they need it in our clients bank account as of closing. After closing, the gift can be returned!!

Total Assets Required: This would be the final amount of Cash To Close, and any Cushion required by the lender.

Section 4; Good Faith Estimate Of Closing Costs

Loan Origination Fee: Our favorite fee--this is part of our payday. Usually 1% of the Loan amount. If charging more, most lenders will have the additional fees charged either as an origination fee or broker fee. Very seldom will they allow it as a "discount". NOTE: On Home Equity Loans, usually all fees are charged on this line--say 3%!!

Loan Discount/Broker Fee: Loan Discount is used for a temporary or permanent buy down by the lender. The Broker Fee is for additional front end fees that you are charging and the buyer is accepting. The Broker is not allowed, except in certain limited circumstances to charge a Discount Fee.

Appraisal: Usually $350 on owner occupied homes, but $450 for investment properties. This is to determine **market value,** not in lieu of an inspection.

Credit Report: For generating a current credit report and updates.

Application Fee: Sometimes used instead of a Credit Report fee.

Good Faith Estimate Of Closing Costs:

Loan Origination Fee	$_____
Loan Discount/Broker Fee	_____
Appraisal	350
Credit Report	75
Application Fee	75**
VA Funding Fee / HOA Transfer	75
Settlement Fee	150**
Document Preparation	225
Title Insurance (Add 1% for refi's)	175
Recording Fees	75
Survey	375
Inspections	_____
Processing Fee	425**
Underwriting Fee (Add $400 for subprime)	150**
Tax Service Fee	150
Messenger Fees	100
TOTAL ESTIMATED FEES	$_____

**SELLER PAYS ON FHA/VA LOANS

VA Funding Fee / (OR) HOA Transfer Fee: Since so few VA loans are done now, I combined with the HOA transfer fee that is on 90% of all loans. The **VA Funding Fee** is 2% of the loan amount, unless the VA entitlement has been used before, then it's 3%.

The **HOA Transfer Fee** is usually in the $50-$75 range, and is charged by the HOA to document the new owner.

Settlement Fee: Charged by the title company to sit in their palatial offices. On a **refi,** this fee could be twice as high as indicated--so watch this!!

Document Preparation: Attorney's fees for preparing closing documents.

Title Insurance: This is for the **MORTGAGEE'S Title Policy,** which covers the mortgage company. In Texas, on resale (used) properties, the seller NORMALLY pays the **Owners Title Policy** that covers the new and old owner, although it is not mandatory, just customary. On new homes and refinances it is customary that the buyer or owner pays the title policy. READ THE CONTRACT!!! Any title company can give a chart on title fees, since they are set by the State, but estimating 1% of the purchase price is a fair estimate to start. **NOTE**: On Texas Cash-out Loans--this fee will be about 25% more for the mandatory state fees, so estimate 1.25% of the loan amount!

Recording Fees: To record documents downtown, usually $3.00 p/page.

Survey: To record the boundary lines, and note any encroachments, easement and restrictions on the use of the property.

Inspections: This is not normally mandatory by the lender, but most buyers will have the home inspected by a qualified inspector or engineer. Many times we don't put anything in this space, just simply point out that the inspection fee is not part of our estimate, since we don't require an inspection.

Processing Fee: Fee for processing the mortgage loan paperwork.

Underwriting Fee: Charged by the lender to evaluate and approve the loan.

NOTE: Add additional for sub prime loans.

Tax Service Fee: To transfer the property tax information from the previous owner to the new buyer.

Messenger Fees: This is a combination of Title Company, Lender and Broker delivery fees. May not be enough in some instances.

Total Estimated Fees: Total of Closing Costs. Total is entered in Section 3 above.

Section 5; Estimated Prepaids

Interest Adjustment: Purchases, use 15 days interest. **Refinances**, use 30 days interest. To calculate: say $100,000 loan @ 6% = $250 (Purchase), or $500 (Refi).

Tax Escrow: Purchases: Use 3 months of estimated or known taxes. Adjust as needed when the tax certificate arrives from the title company. **Refinances:** Escrow for the number of months used in the year **PLUS** three months in order to build up enough reserve to pay the full years taxes in December. EX; Refi closing in July, collect 7 (used), + 3 (new) reserve months, or 10 total months to go into the escrow account at the new lender.

Proof: Closing in July, no August payment. Then payments in September, October, November and December. These 4 payments added to the 10 set up when closed = 14 total months in escrow. In December, lender pays 12 months of taxes, net effect is still 2 months tax reserve remaining.

ESTIMATED PREPAIDS

Interest Adjustment 30 / 15 days est $	_____
Tax Escrow - 3 months	_____
Hazard Insurance - 14 Months	_____
PMI - 2 Months	_____
HOA (Months remaining)	_____
TOTAL PREPAIDS-est.	$ _____

Hazard Insurance: Always maintain 14 months of insurance or cash for compliance. **Purchase:** Borrower will have sent to title company a 12 month policy to be paid at closing. Lender will reserve two additional months. **Refinances:** The remaining policy life, and new cash escrowed will equal 14 months insurance premiums. So, closing in July, and the policy expires in December, equals fives months remaining life. Then escrow new funds for nine months, totaling 14 months of policy life and cash.

PMI: Escrow two months of cost. Not required on sub prime.

HOA: Normally paid in January for the current year in advance. **Purchase:** Calculate the remaining cost due to the current owner, since it has been prepaid. EX: Closing June 30th, with a monthly cost of $25. Current owner would be reimbursed 6 months X $25 = $150 for the remainder of the year. **Refinances:** Unless unpaid at time of refinancing, not calculated because current owner is also borrower.

Total Prepaids-Est: Total of Prepaids. Total is entered in Section 3 above.

YSP: These are back end fees paid by the lender to the Broker for services rendered.

Section 6; Signatures/Dates

All borrowers and the LO sign and date this document. Make a copy for the borrower.

☐ I/WE hereby acknowledge receipt of this disclosure and the HUD Guide for Home Buyers

BORROWER	DATE CO-BORROWER DATE

Loan Officer _____ Date _____

Truth In Lending (TIL):
See Appendix for an example.
See Appendix for items to include as Prepaid Finance Charges (PFC)

The purpose of the TIL is so the consumer can compare the final and total Annual Percentage Rate (APR) of many different lenders and brokers using interest rate, and fees as the parameters. In reality, this is one of the most confusing forms a borrower, lender, broker and attorney will ever be confronted with in their working life!

This document must be signed, faxed or delivered to borrowers within 3 business days of completion of the loan application. No Exceptions. If mailing the document, keep a copy for your records, and make a note of the date mailed to borrower.
I recommend completing or having the document completed at application.

The APR is always higher than the NOTE rate!

In fact years ago, I was working on a project and decided that I wanted to learn more about TIL's. I made up a loan scenario, and sent it to four different attorneys that specialized in real estate. I received four different answers as to the Annual Percentage Rate from the TIL! I became convinced that the TIL was one of the most asinine documents invented, and my opinion hasn't changed!

In completing this document, on the GFE, you will input all the Prepaid Finance Charges (PFC) that the buyer or others are responsible for in their transaction. These PFC items are then subtracted from the total (actual) loan amount to determine the loan amount on the TIL.

The TIL calculation will be computed with the proper PFC items included. Ultimately, the TIL will identify the following items of importance:
- APR-Cost of Annual credit
- Finance Charges-Total of finance charges if paid to full term
- Amount Financed-Loan amount, less PFC items
- Total of Payments-Total of all payments if paid for full term

The TIL will also show the monthly payments with and without Mortgage Insurance.
There are also a series of questions and answers to complete for each TIL. Most of these can be templated on your Processing Software. Then simply answer the other questions as determined by whether the loan is a fixed rate, adjustable, with or without a balloon.

Have the borrower sign and date the document.

Onward we go, learning more how to be a highly paid professional mortgage loan officer!

If you have an interest in joining this dynamic team, call 281-445-1901, X204 for the "President's Hotline"
or
Email: Wes@TexasSupremeMortgage.com

Marketing!

Marketing yourself as a Loan Officer takes many forms, and needs to be consistent so that the income stream remains strong and constant. Just being visible is a starting point.
Each marketing idea in this chapter has been used and proven by myself and other loan officers that have been employed by my company. These ideas are not "pie-in-the-sky", marketing ideas but proven techniques and systems.

I can guarantee that by employing these ideas, your business will be strong and stay consistent until you choose to market yourself, "By Referral Only"! You will work very hard the first six months getting your business started. This can equate to getting a Boeing 747 off the ground for flight. The plane will expend an enormous amount of energy to take off, but once it is at "cruising" altitude, it still requires energy, however much less than in the takeoff mode!

This is the take off mode!

75% of new Loan Officers do not make a living long-term in this business. The past few years since 2000 have been wonderful years in lending. However, this "low hanging fruit of refinances", may soon be diminished. Every loan officer needs a consistent mix of purchase, new home and refinance business. Following these marketing techniques and systems will help you to be one of the 25% that make a good living in this business.

The following guide and marketing ideas are designated for the takeoff mode, not for the rest of your life. Remember, a loan officer can succeed quite well with a small group of Realtors or real estate agents consistently referring their purchase clients to you.

Basic Realtor Marketing

Breaking The Ice!
1) Locate approximately 30 realtor offices, yes 30 offices. Map these out so that you can efficiently find and drive to these offices. My approach is to go to 15 offices daily, and rotate these offices every other day. Monday, Wednesday and Friday will be a "set" of offices and Tuesday, Thursday and Saturday will be the second "set" of offices. Every two weeks, change the days that you go to each group of offices. This will insure that you see different people at the offices. The only variation on this grouping might be to go to all 30 offices on Monday, since the majority of Realtors have their office meetings on Tuesday mornings. If this time is spent well, the dividends will pay off for the long run in repeat and predictable business.

2) The first time that a new office is approached in a cold call method, there are several important steps to consider and remember. Your being there is an interruption to the receptionist's day. You will want to make her your friend and confidant quickly. She is the gatekeeper for the office, and consequently your biggest ally, or worst enemy! Make her your

friend by being friendly to her and asking for her advice, help and permission to continue to call on the office.

3) The first time you actually get the nerve to enter the office area, smile big and extend your hand to her and introduce yourself. The receptionist will tell you her name, remember it, and repeat it back to her. I would always ask for a business card of the Broker, and on the back write down her name and physical attributes. This will help you remember the different receptionist in each office, since you now have 30 to remember.

4) After this brief introduction, ask her a few basic questions. I would always have my flyers that I was distributing to each Realtor in my hand, and simply ask her where the mailboxes were, and indicate that I will be glad to stuff them because I know she's busy. Act as if you belong there, and you want to sincerely help her with this job! Tony Robbins wrote; "Confidence comes before competence!" In this instance, if you act confidently and act like the professional mortgage person you are, very few people will not want to help you!

Most large real estate offices are now associated with a mortgage company. The real estate broker will have some inducement to the real estate agents to use the "in house mortgage person". However, my experience has been that the agents usually resist this and detest using the in-house mortgage company. They usually resist because the real estate agents are very territorial in determining where the loan is placed, and they feel that the in-house person is forced on them, and does not earn his rewards by actually generating the loan. No more than 25% of transactions are placed with the in-house mortgage person; therefore 75% of all purchase transactions are now available for you!

In addition to the above sentiments of the real estate agents, I've always wondered why the Realtor would risk 3-6% of the sales price, their commission, to gain a few dollars, or some token reward by using an in-house mortgage company they did not like anyway! It doesn't make financial or business sense, and may be a violation of RESPA anyway!

5) Once you have stuffed the mailboxes with your flyers, and made small talk with anyone you encounter, thank the receptionist for her time and tell her you will see her later in the week. Specific flyer strategy will be discussed later.

6) The second time I walked in, I would smile big and say, "Hi Mary, Wes, it's been a whole two days since I saw you last, My-O-My, you're looking good as usual". Begin to act as if you "own" the office. Treat it as if you are "an actor on stage", and everyone is paying rapt attention to only you, because they will be. Each visit, make small talk with the receptionist, and begin asking her probing questions that she can easily answer. I would begin with casual conversation regarding asking along this line of discussion:
- Who is the top producer this month?
- Who is consistently a good producer of closed loans?
- Who would she want to work with, if she were a loan officer like me?
- Who would she avoid working with?
- Who is having trouble with their current loan officer now?

- Anyone's listing not closing because of lending "opportunities"?

Keep in mind; this is not an inquisition, but just a casual conversation between two "old friends". These questions are intended to get her to open up with useful information, so that it will be beneficial to the office and yourself.

This second or third visit to the office is a great time to have her introduce you to an agent or two. The receptionist now can trust that you will be returning **consistently**. Once again, just make small talk with the agent, but get some critical information from the agent also. This group of questions to the agent would be as follows:

- How long have you been a real estate agent?
- Do you enjoy the business?
- What made you decide to become an agent?
- How do you generate your business?
- Do you remember the last loan officer you chose for a purchase transaction?

(Surprisingly, 80% or more will not remember the name of the last loan officer they worked with)

- What is important in your relationship with a loan officer?
- Would you mind if I email you some information each week on lending?
- Would you work with me if I could provide your clients great service, return your

phone calls, tell you and your clients the truth and have fair interest rates?

This business is not rocket science. When these six steps are repeated on a consistent basis, your business will begin to prosper. The key is to continue so that the real estate agents know they can depend on your consistency, timeliness and accountability. This will help to insure that they come to depend on you as a resource.

One note of caution; the turnover rate of receptionists in real estate offices is tremendous. When you walk in as described in #6, and "Mary's" no longer employed, now what?

Use this approach and you will be great; as you walk in and notice that's not Mary, you look at the new receptionist, and declare, "You're not Mary, where's Mary (my old friend)? If this new person is now the new "Mary", introduce yourself, smile big and gently inform her that you have the run of the office and already know where the mail boxes are, so you will gladly insert your flyers for the benefit of the agents! If she's a temporary person, the stage is still yours. Ask when Mary is returning, so that when Mary does return, you can comment how much you missed her!

In this environment, it is best to learn how to roll with the punches and go with the flow as they say! Some real estate offices have a closed door policy. This is just a challenge to success, not a detriment to your long-term success.

In my 7 years of consistently calling on real estate offices, I was asked to leave a couple of offices for taking too much for granted or for having too much "fun" in the bull-pen area while the agents were just "hanging out." Once, I and about six agents were having a great time on a Thursday afternoon. Telling jokes and generally just laughing and relaxing.

This office had about 50 agents, and I was entertaining them with my jovial disposition and regaling them with stories of past funny stories of lending (all confidential of course). Some of these are included in a later chapter.

They were all in stitches—I was "on stage"! In the distance, the new office manager comes barging out of her office, and points back to me, and bellows;

"You, Mr. Loan Officer, come here right now!"

I hear a collective "oh no", under the breath from the six agents!

As I'm walking briskly, yet sheepishly to the manager's side, I'm smiling broadly and trying to act like I "own the place"—she's having none of that this afternoon. "You, Sir, she states, are disturbing my agents, my office and myself, and are to leave immediately, and not return until further notice!" Yes Maam, and out the door I go! Yikes—that is one of my best and most productive offices!

I had to plan my next move, because I couldn't have a problem with that particular office. The next morning about 10:30, I show up, and ask the receptionist, my old friend, how's "Janet" (the office manager) today? Not too good she informs me! **Gulp!**

I had bought and brought one long-stemmed red rose, and a small box of chocolate covered cherries. The manager's office was just past the reception booth, I asked the receptionist to say a small prayer, "I'm going in"! So I eased up to the manager's office and stuck the long-stemmed red rose thru the door so she could see it, I poked my head around the corner and cheerfully, asked, "Can I come in?" Invited in, I then apologized for the disruption the day before. I indicated that I knew I could get loud and boisterous, but truly meant no harm to her production. We shared the chocolate covered cherries!

No harm, no foul!

There's a very important point in this story though. If you have a problematic situation in an office with a real estate agent or manager, it must be addressed quickly or you will lose the nerve to recapture the office. The longer you wait, the harder it gets to return to the office. So as Tony Robbins proclaims; "Action Cures Fear"!

> *Remember, we are going through all of these trials and tribulations because we have to get our Boeing 747 airborne!*
> *It is not for the rest of your life!*

Follow-Up Strategies and Techniques To Attract Real Estate Agents!

7) **Quote Sheets**: Many loan officers will hit the streets with quote sheets daily. I must admit, the first month in the business, I did the same. Then I quickly determined that if all you have to offer is "rate", then you have nothing really to offer. Some other loan officer or company will offer an 1/8th of a point less and you're out of the loan. You never want to consistently be in a downward bidding war to secure a loan or a client. Even though the public and media may perceive the mortgage lending industry as a commodity, there is a huge difference in service between mortgage brokers and lenders.

I do not recommend this strategy!

8) **Donuts:** If you want to see a feeding frenzy, bring a couple of dozen donuts to a realtor office at 10AM! There is blood in the water for the sharks to feed on! Actually, this idea has some merit, just be sure that your business cards are attached to the box when leaving the donuts in the work room or lunch room. Even better is to actually walk around the office and offer a selection to each real estate agent that is there! Of course you are making small talk and handing out your card or flyer at the same time.

9) **Candy Jar:** This was one of my long-term favorite marketing ideas that worked consistently for years. I would purchase a "sun tea" jar, tape my business card on the inside of the lid, inside and bottom of the jar. I would then fill the sun tea jar with hard candy, and leave a few more loose cards inside the jar. Each week, I would refill the jar.

I purchased these jars for under $3.00 and about $3.00 worth of candy per jar each week.

These jars would almost always be located in the work or lunch rooms, so when refilling my jar, I would visit with whoever was there, and put flyers in the mailboxes! I ended up with 27 offices that had my sun tea jars, and was ultimately known for a while as "The CandyMan"!

During this period, there were several ideas that kept this technique fresh.

For instance, after a closing, I would fill up the jar with "chocolates", and attach a sign:

"Thanks to Sally Smiths' Closing, Your Office Receives Chocolates This Week"!

At Christmas, I would purchase "Santa" sun tea jars for the season, and give them away after Christmas to a deserving agent. Some months I would run a "special", that said for any agent that closed a loan thru me, they would get their very own special candy jar full of chocolates!

The benefit of these jars and the candy was, 1) It forced me to be in the office on a regular basis, 2) It gave me a reason to wander back to the "inner sanctum" and refill the jars, 3) My name was always in front of the agents either in the work or lunch room, and finally, 4) No one else in my marketplace had anything similar in place.

Finally, I would get sort of "anal" about my jars! Occasionally, a receptionist would not allow me to go refill the jar myself. If I was not allowed to go back and refill my jars myself, I would take out the jar and tell the manager why. "My jars needed to see me each week, because they were lonely for, "The CandyMan"!" Almost 100% of the time, the manager would let me leave the jar, and tell the receptionist, that, "Wes was the exception" to the rule! That's how I ended up with 27 jars in 30 offices!

That's because I acted like I owned the place!

10) **Sponsor a Realtor Open House:** Many weeks, the agents after their Tuesday morning meeting will tour the new listings or several homes, usually with food at each home. I would offer to sponsor the drinks, and a door prize. Be careful if you are volunteering that you do not get "volunteered" to pay for a $500 catered lunch, like I did ONCE!

By sponsoring the drinks and a door prize, you get to meet and greet many agents from several different offices. Open house tours usually last 2 hours. I would choose a heavy glass bowl as a door prize. As the agents come in, collect their business cards in the bowl or have them complete a coupon for the big drawing at the end of the open house. At the end of the event, select the winning agent for the door prize.

If the winning agent is present, present them with the bowl, and take their picture receiving the prize. If they are not present, deliver the bowl that afternoon to their office, and make a big deal out of the agent winning the prize at the open house you sponsored!

11) **Long-Stem Red Roses**: Who doesn't like long-stem red roses? Not any lady I have ever met. Get a dozen of these long-stemmed red roses, and wrap each one individually in the green tissue paper. There are two methods with this technique.

Sometimes, I would give one **only** to the receptionist, my old friend, in each office!
She would remain my loyal friend and friendly gatekeeper for a long time thereafter.
Other times, I would come armed with a dozen long-stemmed red roses for **each lady** I saw in the office, starting with the receptionist, until there were no more roses left.

There was a florist not far from my home that sold long-stem red roses for $6.98 p/dozen.
It is not hard to imagine the BUZZ in the office after I departed!

12) **Mortgage Payment Schedules:**   Offer to work up a mortgage payment schedule using 3 or 4 different scenarios. Be sure to include a schedule of cash to close also. This will give potential buyers the monthly payment, and cash requirements for closing.

I would typically use a little above market interest rates for this schedule. The type of financing demonstrated should depend on your market. However, I would include a FNMA 30 and 15 year fixed rate, and 2/28 Sub-prime at the least. Make several flyers to leave in the home, and also in the sign box outside!

Be sure to input the loan information thru your processing software, to establish an APR for meeting RESPA guidelines. There are several good software programs that make this task easy to complete. Use the Prepaid Finance Charge worksheet listed in the Appendix.

A variation of this mortgage payment schedule is to "borrow" one of the Realtor's flyers from the sign mailbox, and on the back (blank) side, copy your payment schedule. Make 30 additional copies, and return them to the mailbox, and send one or deliver it to the agent with a note, "Dear Agent; I have provided several copies of this flyer in your sign mailbox on 1234 Main Street, Any Town, TX, 77067! I hope you and I can work together on this home sale"!

In this instance, you are taking the approach that it is better to ask forgiveness than permission! Most agents will not mind, but every so often one will mind. If it is a problem, offer to remove the flyers with your information.

13)   **Handwritten Notes:**   Many newspapers and industry publications will list accomplishments and promotions of real estate agents in their office or organization.
The accomplishment could be for an office promotion, new job assignment, top sales award or even a news article on a community function or an article about a vacation the agent had recently taken. Write a handwritten note on each event and send it to the agent. In this note, you are both congratulating them on their promotion, and asking to work with them on future mortgage needs. Create a database to keep in touch with these agents. Email and snail mail follow up information on a consistent recurring basis.

14)   **Women's Council of Realtor and Monthly Association Meetings**:   Attend as many of these events as you possibly can. They usually last 1-2 hours, and you can network with agents that you would not ordinarily be meeting in their "closed" offices. Hand out your cards and any flyers that you may have, if allowed!

15)   **Tuesday Caravans:**   This is a variation of the Realtor Open House (#10). Each Tuesday, many agents still tour the new listings. Offer to drive a group of them in your automobile or SUV!   **HINT:** If you're driving a 1964 Dodge-this may not work for you!

By offering to drive, you now have the undivided attention of several agents in your auto. This is a great networking tool.

16)   **Feed Them:**   Offer to buy breakfast or lunch for agents that you are cultivating.
I remember listening to Gregg Frost; from Albuquerque, New Mexico in 1993 tell a story that one of his main marketing techniques was to take a different agent to breakfast and lunch each day for an entire quarter. He would then repeat for the next quarter.

This method would ensure that each quarter you met one-on-one with 44 agents monthly, and 132 agents' quarterly, assuming 22 work days monthly! If you compute the incremental cost of breakfast at $10 each, and lunch at $15, the expense would be $25 daily more than eating alone. This $550 expense will pay off handsomely in current and future benefits. One new transaction a year and the incremental cost are covered.

Additionally, by working with and prearranging these meetings at the same restaurant for the quarter, I'm quite sure they would give a discount, and treat you and your guest like the King and Queen you are! This could be set up with a special table, so that upon arrival, you are ushered in to your designated spot.

17) **Sponsor the Realtor Weekly Meeting:** Most offices have a weekly meeting of all the agents. In some offices, this meeting is "mandatory", however, most offices do not require attendance, but encourage it. It is wise to bring some type of food to this meeting for each agent. Bagels or Donuts are good choices! Watch the feeding frenzy!

At this meeting, offer some brief, specific tips on financing or another tool that the agents can use. However, this lender information is not the main thrust of our presentation.

Every lender that presents on Tuesday morning talks about service, processing, low rates, blah, blah, blah, we've heard this all before (the agents are thinking) a hundred times! The agents quickly become bored to tears!

In my presentations, I'll briefly speak on one specific loan product, and then ask if it's OK to show them how my database of closed clients consistently provides me a six figure income annually without advertising? **This gets their attention!** I'll show them how a $5,000 annual investment consistently returns $400,000 in gross closed commissions without running any advertising. **This gets their attention!** I'll show them how easy it is to set this up and maintain the database, so that at some point we now have a saleable asset of documented consistent referrals from closed clients. **This gets their attention!**

In this meeting, be different than the last 100 lenders that were there. Be educational, entertaining and informative. They will remember you!

I've got good news! The information presented to the agents at their weekly meeting is presented in this book also. It is presented in detail in the chapters; "By Referral Only, The Best Investment I Ever Made and Database Mining for Gold!

18) **Payday Candy Bars:** **After closing**, deliver a Payday candy bar to each agent, with a note that reads as follows; "Thanks for the smooth closing on the Smith transaction. Here's another payday, you can really sink your teeth in".

If you are just soliciting the agents, include a note as follows to the agent; "Here's a small Payday you can sink your teeth in. If you want to insure a real payday, let me be the Loan Officer on your next transaction"!

19) **Millionaire Candy Bars & "$100,000 Grand Candy Bars":** Attach a note for each agent that reads as follows; "Stick with me as your Loan Officer, and I'll see that YOU earn

a Million Dollars this year!" or "I want YOU to earn no less than $100,000 this year! Stick with me and I'll see that you do earn a Hundred Grand"!

Have some fun with the Paydays, Millionaire and $100,000 Grand candy bars! These can be bought in bulk at Sam's Club, Costco and other stores. Just be careful to not eat too many before distributing them and making yourself sick!
Have some fun with these ideas!

FUNNY STORY: Once, I was trying to get into this office for about three months, and never could get past "Jennifer", the 21 year old blond blue eyed, drop dead gorgeous receptionist at this ERA office. She was the "Ice Queen" to me! Each time I would enter the lobby, her eyes would grow cold and as if she was peering thru little slits! I was about to give up, except this office was 5 minutes from my home, and had about 15 agents. Ummm-What to do???

Finally, I found out somehow that it was Jennifer's birthday, and also the Broker's birthday on the very same day. So, on that fateful day, I marched into the office as if I owned it (again), and saw the "Ice Queen"! I walked boldly up to her and summoning all my courage stated in one long sentence, "Jennifer, I heard today was your birthday, and do you know how long I've been coming into this office?" No she say's flatly! "Well I do, it's been three long months and ever since the first day I saw you I wanted to give you a big 'ol juicy kiss, I figured that since today was your birthday, what the heck, today's the day"! (Still not breathing) Now before she could reach back and slap the fire out of me, I reached over and gave her a small bag of Hershey Kisses, while proclaiming, "What the heck, here's 9 big ol kisses from The Dreammaker!"

After what seemed like an eternity (3 seconds probably) she laughed and we became friends for the next year that she worked there!

Little did I know that an 89 cent bag of Hershey Kisses could go so far!

I also gave the Broker, John Leon, a Millionaire candy bar and told him I would help him earn million dollars by using me as their lender. He and I were friends for years, and this became a very productive office!

The point is to never, never give up—find another angle to your success.

---

20) **Realtor Floor Time:** Many agents still spend 2-4 hours weekly, on "floor time", waiting for someone to call on the general office advertising. Offer to sit with the agents, and pre-qualify anyone who calls during this time. This may seem like a lot of time and energy to talk to 2-3 potential clients in this time period. You could go spend your hard earned dollars to run an ad yourself; however, the real estate broker has already spent the money to generate the activity. You are just there to help pre-qualify the new clients.

Again, as a loan officer, you are building up a rapport with the agent you are helping on floor time. You can easily pass the time with regaling the agent with "funny stories" of lending found elsewhere in this book!

In reality, what generally happens is that you get introduced to every agent that wanders in by the agent on duty for floor time. Make it a point to get introduced and spend time with every agent that is in the office. This is a great time to strike up a meaningful conversation with the Broker, Branch Manager or Office Manager.

The point of you being there is to; 1) pre-qualify callers form the ads, 2) build up a rapport with the agent you are directly supporting, 3) meet and greet other office agents, and 4) meet the management of the office.

21) **New Agent Training:** Once you meet and build up a reputation in the agents' office, this is an excellent time to offer to hold an informal meeting with the agents that are just receiving their license. This is why it is important to be introduced to the Broker and manager while helping the agents on "floor time"!

I always found these new agents to come out with a huge amount of energy and a desire to succeed. If you catch these agents early in their career, and train them in the proper method of working with loan officers, you will have a long-term relationship of continuing business. I worked with several agents like this for 10 years, and received almost 100% of their business.

Unfortunately, 80% of all new agents are out of the business in 18-24 months. I always saw that the first six months was the easiest. They were full of energy and desire, yet "reality" hasn't set in yet. These new agents are like young puppies! Running around like crazy, marketing, talking to people and marketing some more! If you can capture some long-term agents here, your business will be consistent. In fact, IF the real estate agent will hook up early with an experienced loan officer that can help them and their clients, it becomes a great long-term partnership!

You might well be the catalyst that keeps the real estate agent in the business for 20+ years!

> **If this seems like too much work and effort to get started, just think how much work and effort it is to be broke, dissatisfied, and unsuccessful?**

22) **Public Open House**: Each Sunday, in some areas, it may be Saturday; the real estate agents have an "Open House" for the public to visit this home. I'm sure you have seen the directional signs in your neighborhood or on major intersections. Follow the signs to meet agents you may have never met, and might not otherwise.

Visit 4 neighborhood open houses for 15 minutes each or less. Usually, you will find a newer agent on the property. The listing agent may have 50 listings, and will assign the open house to a newer agent or their buyer's agent. The new agent is working to get leads, regardless if the lead buys the home the agent is holding as the open house, or another home.

Aren't we all looking for the same buyers?

Your purpose is to meet these agents on Sunday, exchange cards, and offer to pre-qualify any leads on Monday morning. The agent will have a sign in sheet. Have them fax this sheet to you on Monday morning to get started. When I was a young pup, getting started, I would actually supply the agent with a sign in form. Of course, my name and company name was prominently displayed! Just be aware, that many people visiting open houses write down "bogus" information. So your call ratio may only be 50% of the list.

> One method of eliminating or reducing the bogus signups is to offer a gift certificate to a local restaurant to one of the prospects from a drawing. In this instance, work with maybe 10 agents and pool all the sign in sheets to offer the gift certificate. So, as an example maybe 8 people each sign up at 10 open houses, and instead of half being bogus, probably none are fictitious. So for 80 real leads, would it be worth a $50 gift certificate?
>
> You might even get the Realtor's to chip in on this because you are increasing their real prospect count also!

If the agent doesn't fax you the list on Monday morning, call the agent for this information. As you build up agents form prior weeks, remember to call all of them on Monday morning. I used to call this time, "Dialing for Dollars"! Consistency is of paramount importance.

The agents want to know that you will be around, available, and trustworthy!

23) **Give Them Drugs:** One of the most effective marketing tools I used was the most helpful too! I would go to Sam's Club, and purchase a poster board with an assortment of Aspirins, Tylenol, Pepto-Bismol, Alka-Seltzer, etc. These cost under $15. Hang the poster board full of "drugs" in their work room. Underneath the poster board, hang a sign with the following wording in big bold lettering on yellow paper. Use 67# cardstock from Office Depot or Office Max, because it holds up longer without wilting!

> **If You Had Used Wes of Texas Supreme Mortgage On Your Last Loan, Your Tummy Would Not Be Upset Now, And You Would Be At Closing!**

I'm sure you just smiled or laughed, so will the agents. This is a novel and inexpensive method to keep your name in the forefront. Of course, additional information on the sign would be your contact information.

24) **Sign Riders for Financing:** Attaching a sign to the agent's real estate sign that offers a certain type of financing, and directs the buyers to a toll free number for more information

is an excellent method of obtaining leads. Be careful not to put any RESPA triggers on the sign without also disclosing the APR, and any other pertinent required information. Most mortgage companies use the guideline of offering a ZERO Down product that does not trigger the RESPA disclosure on the sign. However, putting $0 Down on the sign would be a RESPA trigger, and would entail disclosing APR, rate, term, payment and other disclosures right on the sign.

So a small difference can make a big difference!

We will discuss the details of signage in the chapter, "By Referral Only, The Best Investment I Ever Made"!

25) **Email Marketing Newsletter:** Now that you have hundreds of real estate agents names and information, start a database so that you can contact them easily and inexpensively via email. This newsletter does not take the place of personal contact. It is an additional method of disseminating your information out to the real estate agents. In this newsletter, you want to offer tips on financing and a generally positive outlook on life. Be sure to give the receiver a chance to opt out of your newsletter, if so desired. However, if your newsletter is disseminating useful information in a positive manner, this will be a rare occurrence. For those that want to opt out—good riddance!

My email newsletter is named; "Monday Marketing". Do not put useless information like Aunt Gertrude's' recipes, gossip or even non-related news stories. Stick to useful and positive information, and they will look forward to seeing your "Monday Marketing" newsletter arrive in their email inbox!

Remember, we are going through all of these trials and tribulations because we have to get our Boeing 747 airborne!
It is not for the rest of your life!

Other Types Of Marketing

26) **Never Throw A Magazine Away Again:** How many old magazines have you thrown away in the last 20 years? A bunch I presume, or recycled the magazines at the recycler, doing your civic duty. Stop doing that, and start doing it my way. Take your address label off, and tape the following message on the magazine:

**This Magazine Provided Free
by
Wes Cordeau; "The Dreammaker"
Texas Supreme Mortgage, Inc.
Cell: 713-899-0091
If You Want A Home Now, Call Wes!
Many Home Loans ZERO Down!
(PS: It's OK to take ME Home!)**

Again, print this card on yellow 67# cardstock, with black lettering. I use the business card setting in Microsoft. The key is just get it accomplished quickly and efficiently!

Whenever you go, the Dentist, Doctor, Nail Salon, Car Wash, etc., wherever there is someone waiting, leave a magazine or two or three in the lobby. This is the most inexpensive method of getting your name out to the public. It's virtually free!

27) **Upwardly Mobile Executives**: In each Sunday paper and in the local business journal is a section listing local promotions of executives receiving promotions, or new jobs. Find the address of each one, and send them a congratulatory letter at work, with the request for helping them with their mortgage needs. There is a very simple three step approach: 1) "Google" the company name listed in the paper, and find the address and phone number of the newly promoted executive. 2) Write a letter of congratulations, 3) Follow up with a phone call within 3 days of mailing the letter. Offer your services, and ask for an email address to keep them abreast for current mortgage trends, and other information. Email weekly, call monthly, and snail mail quarterly. You always want to be top of mind consciousness to the executive.

28) **Work with Human Resources Directors**: Sometimes, you will get "lucky", and have a promotion for a director of Human Resources. This can be a goldmine! The HR Director has access to personnel moving in and out of the city, and can give you access to valuable information. Obviously, they cannot give out any personal information about their employees, however the following list is an example of the help the HR Director could easily give you for their employees:
- Allow a payroll "stuffer" in each employee's pay envelope to advertise your services, and products. Keep this simple. One product at a time.
- Allow you to hold a home buying seminar at lunch, end of the work day, or even on a Saturday for the employees and their families.
- Write an article in the company newsletter on the benefits of homeownership.

In return, maybe you could offer a prize at the home buying seminar, or a discount for employees: Call the discount, "The Acme Widget and Buggy Whip Company Discount"!

Another idea is to offer to donate $100 to the coffee club for each closing, each article written or each home buying seminar held. Watch for RESPA guidelines on this though.

29) **For Sale By Owners (FSBO's):** In each newspaper there are virtually hundreds of sellers that need your help. There is also a FSBO magazine and a specialty website, www.FSBO.com, where there are hundreds more sellers desperately trying to sell their home. Also, there is www.CarltonSheets.com that has hundreds of listings of properties FSBO! We, as mortgage professionals have all the tools necessary to help them administer the sale of their home. This is virtually a free marketplace, and the FSBO's are desperately looking for help, they just don't know it yet.

Here's why they don't know it yet!

The typical FSBO is trying to save a little money, maybe 6% of the sales price. Guess what, every potential buyer who calls the FSBO thinks they will save 6%, because there's no real estate agent involved! Ultimately, they may split the difference, and each saves 3%! But, it can be a pure headache to save this 3%!

The FSBO is actively marketing his property, installing a FSBO sign in his yard, placing ads in the newspaper, flyers on grocery store bulletin boards, flyers at work in the break room, maybe the FSBO magazine, and any other outlets he can find. The FSBO is a "marketing genius", he thinks! Then what! What we have discovered is that even though the FSBO is a marketing whiz, and finds a buyer that's interested; the FSBO ultimately doesn't really know what to do once some one says, "I want to buy your home!"

I equate this moment to, **"a dog chasing a car"!** We've all watched dogs chase cars! Woof, Woof, Woof! The dog is chasing (marketing) as hard as possible. Then the car suddenly stops! The dog can't eat the car, so he stops and walks away. The dog doesn't know what to do with a car he's just caught! The thrill was in the chase!

This is our FSBO too!

We as mortgage professionals have all the tools to help the FSBO!

We have regular access to:

- Attorneys that can help them prepare the contracts and documents inexpensively
- Agents or Brokers that will help them write the contracts for a small fee
- Title Companies to facilitate the closing
- Insurance agents for property insurance
- Appraisers to determine market value
- Survey companies to identify boundaries and easements
- Inspectors and information regarding necessary inspections
- Our mortgage company for a mortgage, both for the buyer of their home, and potentially for the FSBO's new home

This is not meant to be a fully inclusive list of contacts we have access to, but the majority of transactions will include at least these service providers listed above. Almost no FSBO will have the same knowledge and access to these providers as we have due to our extensive professional knowledge.

FSBOs are a huge market for purchase transactions. The cost can be virtually free.

How do I get to the FSBO marketplace?

This is a four step process that has proven over and over again to produce results.
29-1) Locate all the FSBOs you want to call from the newspaper or magazine.

29-2) Call their home on your cell phone. If they are at home, the following dialog will work perfectly:

> Ring, ring; Hello, I'm calling about your home for sale! They will usually ask your name, give it to them clearly. Then they will tell you about the home; three bedrooms, two baths, 2,500 square feet, etc. **Make Notes!** Inquire about the price, property taxes, insurance, home owner's association fees, etc. **Make Notes!** Ask them what neighborhood the home is in. Finally ask them the address of the property. (PS; If this was a good enough price, you actually might want to buy this as an investment or homestead for yourself)

> If the FSBO is not home, simply leave your name and cell phone number only, and tell them you are interested in the home they have advertised for sale in the newspaper. Do not leave your company name at this point in time. Then follow the same procedure as when they were home when you are able to actually speak with the FSBO.

> About this time, the FSBO may ask you if you are a, "Realtor", in a combative tone! They usually have received 50 calls from real estate agents trying to get their listing. Assure them that you are not a "Realtor" trying to get their listing, however we do have something for FREE that will help them sell their home!

> Ask the FSBO if they mind us sending for free, something of value that will help them sell their home and make them sleep easier at night! This will get their attention!

> **Be forewarned, that 2% of the people will get angry because you did not identify yourself right upfront as a mortgage professional.**

> Don't argue with these 2%, just say, I'm sorry, if you don't want my information for free, that's ok, I understand and move on to the other 98% that will love you and your information. These 2% are the same people you see arguing at

the grocery store that the tomatoes are not ripe enough, or too ripe! Move On!

29-3) Mail the free packet of information to the FSBO:
Once they have given the OK for mailing, send a packet of information via regular or overnight mail to them. You might double check to be sure that the address given above is their mailing address also. In this packet you will have the following information:
- Letter offering our services and a list of types of providers that are necessary to have a successful transaction
- Customized spreadsheet showing 3-4 types of financing for their home
- Sign up form to record their incoming leads for the sale of their home. These prospects are to be called or faxed to our office daily or weekly.
- List of items required for loan application
- Map to our office
- Mini-Application for a pre qualification application
- Business Cards
- Any type of "trinkets", notepads, pens, bookmarks, etc with your name
- Picture of available free FSBO sign for their yard (Optional)

The benefits we can offer, as mortgage professionals are tremendous. We can gain the trust of the FSBO by offering a solution to their needs, and a smooth transaction in an area that we have much needed expertise. Our knowledge is of paramount importance to the FSBO, and their buyers.

Another huge, but seldom thought of benefit for the FSBO is security and safety. The police will confirm that some "buyers" that are looking at the FSBO's home aren't really looking at the home, as much as they are looking at the "stuff" in the home. The bad guys can check out the security alarm, lighting and note where the most valuable and easily removable items are located. Generally, the FSBO will give the "buyer" access to all areas of the home and closets in showing the home. This is an open invitation to the bad guys! The bad guys can easily unlatch a downstairs window latch in 2 seconds while the FSBO is not paying much attention, but trying to market the home to this "buyer".

> YES, some people are actually casing the home for a return visit!
> No FSBO takes this into account, because they are "chasing the car"! Woof, Woof, Woof!

If the FSBO will let us pre-qualify every caller, and report the results, this action will tremendously lessen the chance of an unscrupulous buyer just looking at their stuff. The buyer will know we have all his information. It is best that we meet face to face with the buyer, because we want to build a rapport with them anyway for this or other lending transactions. After all is said about this security though, **be very careful** not to over-promise that we are a security company and can confirm or guarantee that the potential buyer is not a security risk. It just lessens the chance of that event by analyzing the buyer before he visits the home.

29-4) Call the FSBO three days after mailing the packet to determine they received the packet and offer to meet with the FSBO, and go over the details of the FSBO sign, and call capture information. The call capture system is a toll free number. The prospective purchasers can call 24 hours daily to receive information on the home, and find out basic information on financing that is available. The buyer can leave a message, or have the associated loan officer paged, or simply hang up after listening to the message. Regardless, the loan officer captures the phone number of the caller. The loan officer can now return the call, and get additional information. Usually, we will have one extension number assigned to each home.

> This four step process is perfect for gaining low cost leads of purchase money buyers. Of course, the buyers that cannot buy the home that they originally called on will be switched to a more appropriate home, and assigned a friendly real estate agent to find them a home!

30) **Internet Website**: There are thousands of methods to create a website and promote it so that clients can find it, and use the website for a mortgage transaction. This is an area that you will need expert help for setup and guidance.

31) **Purchase Internet Leads**: If you "Google", "Purchase Internet Mortgage Leads", you will get 256,000 items available. Some people swear by purchasing leads, and some people swear at the lead sellers!

32) **Flyers in Homes Magazines:** This is an extremely low cost method of marketing. Simply go into the grocery store where all the home magazine racks are located, and insert your flyer into the middle of each magazine. Use 67# Cardstock paper. Use one half of a letter sized flyer, so that it will easily insert while you are standing in front of the magazine rack. (PS: Bail money is not included with this marketing tip)

33) **Write Articles**: Write an article for your neighborhood gazette or local newspaper. Many times these magazines could use someone to write basic articles on the mortgage market in your area. Once you become an "author", you are now the expert! At the end of the article, you are allowed to include your name, contact and company information.

Although, you would not be allowed to blatantly promote yourself, by virtue of the article, you become the "expert" on mortgages in your area!

34) **Sponsor A Youth Sports Team:** Whether it's soccer, baseball or softball, this is a very inexpensive method of promoting your company. Usually the cost is under $200, and you then have 15-20 young adults wearing your name on their shirts or jersey's.

35) **Coach A Youth Sports Team:** When my children were growing up, I coached their soccer teams for several years. Even though it was a large time commitment, it was well worth the effort. I enjoyed actively being involved with my children, and many parents decided that by transference, if I was as interested in their mortgage loan as I was with coaching their children, that would work well for them.

36) **Join A Neighborhood Church, Social or Political Group**; Being actively involved with something you enjoy will allow you to network with like minded people, and potentially work with these people on their mortgage needs.

37) **Toastmasters/BNI/Lead Exchange Groups;** Join weekly or monthly groups where you can interact and trade leads. These meetings can range from very formal to highly informal. I've been involved with breakfast and lunch groups for lead exchanges. The payoff usually begins within the first four meetings. Don't be discouraged, if it takes that long or more! Keep spreading your message, and the results will follow. Make sure that you have current leads to give also, don't just be a "lead receiver".

In our daily business, we routinely come across people who will need the services of others in the lead group. Our **Reticular Activator System** will be working overtime so that we can generate leads for others. The Reticular Activator System is the same system in your brain that notices ALL the cars just like the one you recently purchased or notices that everyone is pregnant now that you are having a baby too!

38) **Trinkets:** There are literally thousands of items that can be used as promotional items. This can be a simple as ballpoint pens, letter openers, note pads or bookmarks. These trinkets can also be as elaborate as you want. My favorite type of item is something that has a "life", such as magnetic baseball, football or basketball schedules, bookmarks, notepads, baseball caps and golf shirts! Anything with your name prominently displayed for an extended period of time is helpful to keep you at the top of consciousness in the client's minds! I like to use a bookmark, and leave it in the "tube" at the drive thru bank for the next person to take out of the tube.

39) **Stealth Marketing**: I coined the term, "Stealth Marketing", in relation to the mortgage business. This method of marketing is like flying under the radar for a high speed Stealth Airplane! Using this method of marketing can put you in front of a thousand highly interested leads monthly at virtually ZERO cost! **Interested?**

This is a very low cost method of meeting new clients. Each week in the newspaper and on TV there are several advertisements for real estate promoters in town selling their "systems" on buying real estate for less than market value, or obtaining grants to get purchase money for homes, or buying government foreclosed homes. These promoters will usually have 6-8 meetings during the week to promote their system.

I have attended several of these meetings. These meetings will have upwards of 2-300 people in each session. Think about who attends these meetings! These people have at least expressed enough desire about real estate or mortgages to leave the confines of their cozy home or apartment to go to the hotel and sit in a meeting for two hours or more. 99% of the attendees will make no decision concerning the system presented. However, they may very well be interested in a standard type mortgage that we have available.

Your purpose in being there is to meet and greet as many of these people as possible and hand them flyers promoting your company and a product they might be able to actually use! Always print the flyer on yellow paper with black printing. Use both sides of the flyer, and have details on purchase money mortgages and refinances.

The best place to catch the participants is just as they are entering or leaving the hotel or auditorium. Of course, if you also join in the session, you can meet additional people inside the meeting room and at any breaks!

Think of this marketing technique as "drafting" off the promoter of the event. The promoter may not be as interested and excited in you handing out your flyers as you are, however, there is no law against this, and the event is being held in a public place.

Be Bold or Go Home!

40) **Builder Marketing:** Most builders will have a mortgage company that is in an ABA arrangement or a wholly owned entity. We all know that the concessions given to the new home buyers are really "smoke and mirrors", however this is hard to work against. The best method is to become a "Preferred Lender" for the builder and join in on the "smoke and mirror' game! The other side and potentially more lucrative method of obtaining builder business is to get the spin off from the preferred lenders. Many times the preferred lenders will not work as hard to obtain the approvals that an outside mortgage broker will.

The mortgage broker will work hard to close these deals, because we generally have to "earn" the business, not as a gift like the preferred lenders or ABA has available to them thru the builder. Once you have established yourself as a mortgage broker that can get these transactions closed, you may also become the "Preferred Lender" for all the transactions, unless the builder and lender have an ABA arrangement!

41) **Data Base Mining for Gold:** This is such an important aspect of marketing, that it is covered in a separate chapter!

Ultimately, your long-term success will be built on the relationships you form with a select few real estate agents and your prior clients!

Remember, we are going through all of these trials and tribulations because we have to get our Boeing 747 airborne!
It is not for the rest of your life!

Onward we go, learning more how to be a highly paid professional mortgage loan officer!

**If you have an interest in joining this dynamic team, call 281-445-1901, X204 for the "President's Hotline"
or
Email: Wes@TexasSupremeMortgage.com**

Flyers That Work

During the course of my career I have used many different flyers to the general public, Realtors and others to generate business. Some have been wildly successful, some not.

One flyer for refinancing generated 25 closed loans from a 1200 unit mail out. That's a phenomenal return. The same flyer to the same neighborhood, three years later produced ZERO closed loans! In the next few pages are flyers that I have used and an explanation of why using them is to your benefit.

This flyer is used to generate activity from small business owners that have decent credit, and good bank deposits, but tax returns are not reflective of true income.

(Side A)

Mr. Business Owner!

ZERO Down Payment

Makes You A

Homeowner!!

(Turn Me Over To Find Out How)

(Side B)

You Can Buy A Home!!
Yes, You!

- No Tax Returns Required
- Decent, But Not Great Credit Allowed
- 600 Mid FICO Credit Score Is All
- 70% of Bank Deposits Counted as Income
- YES, 70% of Bank Deposits in Last 12 Months
- ZERO Down Payment

Sounds Too Good Bo Be True!

Call: Wes Cordeau today!!
Office: 281-445-1901, x204
Cell: 713-899-0091
(He wrote the book on Mortgages in Texas!)

This Flyer is used with divorce Attorney's to help their clients!

I'm D-I-V-O-R-C-E-D, Now What Do I Do?

Do You Know The Answers To These 11 Important Questions?
(Hint: I do)

1) The house is in both of our names--I don't like that!!   What can I do?

2) I'm living in the house can I get his (her) name off the mortgage?

3) I signed over the Warranty Deed, but my name is still on the mortgage, am I still responsible, if he (she) doesn't pay the mortgage timely?

4)   With my name still being associated with the mortgage, will this impair my ability to buy another home?

5) If my name is still on the mortgage, do I get part of the tax deductions?

6) What can I do to really protect myself from future liability in this situation?

7) I feel helpless. Is there a professional who can advise me on these questions?

8) Will I ever be able to buy another home?   How long, and what is the process?

9) Soon I will have a new spouse. Will this affect me?

10) Is there a waiting period after the divorce is final to either refinance the home or purchase another home?

11) My EX messed up our joint credit.   Will this keep me from buying a home?

Wes Cordeau (MB1021) is a professional mortgage broker. He has been in direct lending since February 1989. **For the last 15 years**, he has dedicated himself to helping families with their housing needs. He has the answers to each and every question above, and can explain the intricacies of the lending process.   Wes has over 60 lenders at his disposal. **From this array of lending sources, there is usually an answer for every situation.**

Call Wes Cordeau @ 281-445-1901 (ofc), 713-899-0091 (cell) for an appointment.

Good, Bad Or Ugly Credit!!   We Can Help!
Full Documentation OR Stated Income!!   We Can Help!!
Purchase or Refinance!!   We Can Help!!
See other side for more information.

This is another low cost-high return flyer!

This flyer is used either for a neighborhood mail out, or on company and public bulletin boards! Always display the notice on yellow paper with black printing for the best eye appeal.

PUBLIC   NOTICE

Interest Rates Are At HISTORIC Lows!!

If you ever thought about refinancing--NOW is the time!!

We can refinance your current mortgage loan and accomplish:

1) No cash to close (minimal cash up front for appraisal/credit)
2) Lower your monthly payment
3) Lower your # of years remaining
4) Put cash in your pocket
5) Skip one months payment

Information Needed:

1) 2001 and 2002 W-2's	5)	Insurance Policy
2) Last two paystubs	6)	Mortgage Statement
3) Last two months bank statements	7)	Current Survey
4) Divorce Decree-if any	8)	Other items as needed

Call: Wes Cordeau, Texas Supreme Mortgage, Inc.

OFC: 281-445-1901
CELL: 713-899-0091

This flyer generated 25 closed refinance loans in a 1,200 home subdivision! Obviously, this rate of return was very good.

Now May Be The Last Time This Century To Refinance Your Home And Lower Your Payment!!

Our computer analyzed your mortgage situation and believes we can lower your monthly payment, lower your term of payout AND in some cases also put cash in your pocket!!

Your loan was one of a few chosen that meet the guidelines that should warrant a refinance. In our analysis of current events, **we feel that interest rates may rise by year** end due to the suffering economy and additional government financing to pay for conflicts and terrorism management.

Even if you are worried about your personal job situation, if you plan to keep the house for three years or more, now is the time to look at refinancing.

Your Current Rate: _____%

Your Current Term: _____Yrs

Let see how low we can go!!

What Do I Need To Do??
Gather the following items:
2 months bank statements for checking, savings and retirement accounts
Last 2 paycheck stubs----1999/2000 W-2's and tax returns
Current insurance policy----Current mortgage statement
Packet of information that you received at closing
Appraisal & Credit Report Money---$425.00*
*Discuss with your loan officer about "rolling" these fees into the new loan.

Call Wes Cordeau
Office: 281-445-1901
Cell: 713-899-0091

PS: Who is the next person you know right now that needs to purchase or refinance a home today.   Please send them to us for service!!

This was an $80,000 gross revenue on a $600 investment!

This goofy little adjustment with the Pizza offer generated a huge amount of business from another neighborhood. This was actually the only time I sent the flyer to the neighborhood—not the third time!

OK!! This is the THIRD time I contacted you!!

What in the heck are you waiting for--A free Pizza??

(Bring this flyer, and I'll send you out some free Pizza-after loan application-:-))

Now May Be The Last Time This Century To Refi Your Home And Lower Your Payment!!

Our computer analyzed your mortgage situation and we believe we can lower your monthly payment, lower your term of payout AND in some cases also put cash in your pocket!!

Your loan was one of a few chosen that meet the guidelines that should warrant a refinance. In our analysis of current events, **we feel that interest rates may rise shortly** due to the suffering economy and additional government financing to pay for conflicts and terrorism management.

Even if you are worried about your personal job situation, if you plan to keep the house for three years or more, now is the time to look at refinancing.

Let's see how we can work together to save you money!!

What Do I Need To Do??
Gather the following items:
2 months bank statements for checking, savings and retirement accounts
Last 2 paycheck stubs----2001/2002 W-2's and tax returns
Current insurance policy----Current mortgage statement
Packet of information that you received at closing
Appraisal & Credit Report Money---$425.00*
*Discuss with your loan officer about "rolling" these fees into the new loan.

Call Wes Cordeau
Office: 281-445-1901, x204
Cell: 713-899-0091
Email: wcordeau@aol.com

This flyer is used for Realtor and real estate agent marketing!

Cookie Cutter, Sound-Alike, Look-Alike Mortgage Companies!!

I **guarantee** that we are not like any you have worked with in the past!!!

Why?? You Ask!!

1) We truly treat all clients like Real People and Friends.
*We **know** that if treated correctly, these clients will refer others to us!!*

2) We try to accurately analyze and assess the client's qualifications.
*We **do not want you wasting** your time on unqualified prospects!!*

3) We take their pictures and give their children a gift at application.
*The application is an **event** to remember and the best way to the parents heart is thru the children!!*

4) After application and prior to closing, we send at least five (5) written communications to the clients.
*We want the client to **feel a part** of the system and **comfortable** with the process!!*

5) One of our loan officers will attend each closing.
*The loan officer has the **expertise** to explain most financial questions that would arise!!*

6) Usually, we bring a special little gift for the clients at closing.
*Closing is a **celebration**!!*

7) Usually, we take pictures of the client and Realtor at closing.
*Closing is a **time for remembrance**!!*

8) After closing, we put their names into our data-base.
*They are now a **part of our system** of monthly communication!! They would receive offers of discounts, scholarship drawings, anniversary letters, etc.*

9) We give parties to our Wholesale Lenders and Reps.
*They help us get **loans approved**!!*

10) We have Fun while performing a detailed technical function.
*If we don't have fun while getting the **job completed**, then it is no fun for anyone!!*

Call Your Favorite Loan Officer: Wes Cordeau

Ofc: 281-445-1901
Fax: 281-445-8805
Cell: 713-899-0091
Email: wcordeau@aol.com
WebSite: TexasSupremeMortgage.com

Who is the next person you know that needs to purchase or refinance a home?

The context of the flyer identifies our strong traits in comparison to the "standard" mortgage brokers and other lenders.
We do things that no other lenders do for the clients!

I used this flyer to introduce a new Loan Officer to the marketplace with specialized knowledge of the credit industry. She was an instant hit! The agents loved the analytical work she could perform for their clients.

You Asked For It We Got It!!

Many Realtors have expressed an interest in having their clients credit situations reviewed. This is to determine the credit worthiness of the applicant.

We Did It!!

We hired the best credit person we could find to service your needs.

Let us introduce:

XXX XXXXX

She has spent 9 years in the Mortgage Credit Reporting industry, working for some of the major credit reporting agencies. She has seen many different credit situations, and knows how to resolve credit discrepancies and help the borrower rebuild their credit history. She can also advise clients on how to increase their FICO credit scores. She has the inside knowledge you need!!

So What!! Why Is This Important To Me??

This will help you get your clients to the closing table and put more revenue in your pocket. By XXX, merging her **extensive credit knowledge** and the **inside mortgage knowledge**, this is a major benefit to *YOU* and your *CLIENT* that no other lender in Houston has!!

Thanks For Bringing This To My Attention!!
How Do I Get In Touch With XXX XXXXX??

XXX XXXXX
Loan Officer
OFC: 281-445-1901
Voice Mail: XXX-XXX-XXXX

We had phenomenal success with this flyer and loan officer; alas, until she got married and moved to another city!

This flyer is mailed with our monthly newsletter. It is on yellow paper with black printing, and a very low cost method of generating leads!

Please post at work!!

Lovely 3-2-2 home for sale!!

Find out how you can purchase a home for ZERO downpayment!

YES!! Zero Down on a lovely home of your own.

Of course, there are some credit restrictions, but call to see if you qualify for a home loan as low as ZERO Down!!

Many other loans available also!!

Wes Cordeau
281-445-1901 (Ofc)
713-899-0091 (Cell)

This flyer consistently generates new leads.

We were responsible for promoting the BY REFERRAL ONLY ½ day seminar. This flyer delivered to 2,000 real estate agents generated hundreds of attendees. In fact we had standing room only, and actually had to turn some late arrivers away at the door!

Come Join Us For Free
You are invited to help us welcome Joe Stumpf of
"BY REFERRAL ONLY".

He is my personal friend and one of the most dynamic
Real Estate marketing trainers available nationwide!!
Wes Cordeau, Texas Supreme Mortgage

Joe and his staff will train you to have a life and a work life!!
Patricia Villarreal, Texas Supreme Mortgage

When: *Monday, October 15th, 2001; 9AM-12Noon*
Where: *Houston Marriott North @ Greenspoint*
              255 N. Sam Houston Pkwy East
              Between Imperial Valley and Greenspoint Dr. on North Side of the
Beltway
Who: *Joe Stumpf, By Referral Only*
Why: *To learn more about marketing and prospering in these*
changing times!
What: *See attached brochure for more exciting details!*

BONUS: *Come early and receive a coupon for a free credit*
              report for your next client and a Guaranteed "Payday"!!*
              *Limited to the first 400 attendees!!
              --You don't want to miss this--
Who is the **next** person you know that needs to purchase or refinance a home?

By helping to sponsor an event of this magnitude, we have an instant recognition and "talking point" with most real estate agents in the future, plus we are recognized on stage at the event! The cost is minimal compared to the returns.

We were giving away credit reports and Payday candy bars to the first arrivals! They were all munching away because of us!

This was one of my all time best flyers when working with real estate agents. It is to the point, and got their attention. I used this many times for repeat business.

CAN YOUR "FORMER" LENDER
GET YOU PAID
ON THIS FILE???

**12 Charge Offs
**3 Good Accounts
**5% Down Payment
**No Escrow Account
**They Are Now Happy Homeowners
**Both Realtors Said: "THANKS Wes!"

WE DID
&
WE WILL FOR YOU!!

CALL: Wes Cordeau
OFC: 281-445-1901
Cell: 713-899-0091

Many times, I would design a flyer using a current newspaper article as a starting point. The article would be related to selling, leadership, current real estate or interest trends, or something that the real estate agents would keep on their desk for more than two minutes.

When I was a little lazy, I would have hundreds of these flyers available to leave with the real estate agents. They could always use a list of items needed for a loan. (See Flyer on P. 67)

ITEMS REQUIRED AT TIME OF LOAN APPLICATION

___CURRENT BANK STATEMENTS – TWO CONSECUTIVE MONTHS - ALL ACCOUNTS-ALL   PAGES(SAME FOR STOCKS, BONDS, RETIREMENT FUNDS & LIFE INSURANCE)
___ADDRESSES FOR ALL BANKING INSTITUTIONS - INCLUDE CORRECT ACCOUNT NUMBERS

___COPY OF MOST CURRENT PAYSTUBS - DATES MUST BE CONSECUTIVE (LATEST 2)

___ SELF-EMPLOYED - TWO YRS. TAX RETURNS & CURRENT P&L

___ SALES CONTRACT - COMPLETED, SIGNED & DATED

___MAILING ADDRESS OF CURRENT EMPLOYER

___PREVIOUS ADDRESS OF EMPLOYER - IF CURRENT EMPLOY IS LESS THAN 2 YRS.

___TWO YEARS W2'S - LATEST 2 YRS.
___LIST OF ALL LOANS PAYABLE - INCLUDE ACCOUNT NUMBERS & MAILING ADDRESS
___RECEIVING A PENSION OR S.S. BENEFITS - COPY OF CHECK OR   AWARD CERTIFICATE
___RECORDED DIVORCE DECREE - EVIDENCE OF CHILD SUPPORT RECEIVED
___OTHER REAL ESTATE OWNED - COPY OF CURRENT LEASES OR RENTAL AGREEMENTS
___RECEIVING GIFT FUNDS - MUST BE IMMEDIATE FAMILY - COMPLETED GIFT LETTER/DOCUMENTATION
___ RENTING - MAILING ADDRESS, NAME OF LANDLORD/APT.COMPLEX, PHONE # OR 12 MO. CANCELLED CHECKS
___CURRENT RENTAL IS UNDER 2YRS. ADDRESSES & NAMES OF ALL PREVIOUS TO TOTAL 2YRS.
___ VA LOANS - COPY OF DRIVERS LICENSE, SOCIAL SECURITY CARDS, ELIGIBILITY CERTIFICATE, CARE EXPENSES
___ RESIDENT ALIEN - COPY OF DRIVERS LICENSE, SOCIAL SECURITY CARDS & GREEN CARDS

MONEY @ APPLICATION:
    APPRAISAL: $ 350.
    CREDIT: $ 75.   505 NORTH SAM HOUSTON PKWY. E.
    APPLICATION FEE: $ 75.   HOUSTON, TEXAS 77060

I AM LOOKING FORWARD TO OUR MEETING ON: Wes Cordeau

_____/_____ OFFICE: (281) 445-1901 FAX: (281) 445-8805
 (Day)   (Time   CELL: 713-899-0091

Now that you have seen several flyers that work, go out and design your own for your own personality. I found the creativity was fun, and then tweaked the flyer for maximum results The main ingredients for producing flyers are to be creative, lively and descriptive so that the format of the flyer is easy to read and understand. Make it have some humor so the flyer will draw the reader's attention and attraction for more than a split second. Make the headline something that will stop the reader and they will want more information.

I like to use the same color combination of a yellow flyer with black printing. This is the most visible color combination to most people.

Have fun with these flyers and change what is not working, and reuse what is working!

Onward we go, learning more how to be a highly paid professional mortgage loan officer!

If you have an interest in joining this dynamic team, call 281-445-1901, X204 for the "President's Hotline"
or
Email: Wes@TexasSupremeMortgage.com

BY REFERRAL ONLY;
The Best Investment I Ever Made!

In November, 1995, a faxed flyer came thru with the headline:

Never Call On A Realtor Again!

That got my attention. Most of my business had been generated from Realtor contacts and their referrals since February, 1989 when I entered the direct lending business, not from client referrals. As stated in the chapter on "Marketing", I knew how to get in the real estate offices, and had fun doing so. Although, 1994 and 1995 had been difficult years in the mortgage business, generally I had made a decent income since entering the business.

However, I was most intrigued by the headline:

Never Call On A Realtor Again!

Within two weeks, the organization, Star Performance Seminars, (the predecessor name to "BY REFERRAL ONLY"), with a man named Joe Stumpf was going to be in town, close to the office for a free half day seminar. I had nothing to lose, let's see what they were talking about! Probably some free donuts and coffee, and maybe meet another Realtor or two!

I joined in on the half day seminar, and was mesmerized by what I was hearing! You could do what? You could operate your business based on what? I had to know more!
At the half-day seminar, I could feel the electricity of the organization. But, it wasn't like a pure motivational seminar that wears off in a few days. There was a real substance that came thru, even in the half-day free seminar – with no donuts, I might add. The overall half-day seminar had the feel of a church revival taught by a preacher that you knew and trusted for years. The only difference was that I had just met Joe and his group of "preachers" that were preaching a method of doing business that was foreign to me and has been a catalyst for a huge increase in my business and quality of life!

They were describing a process that you are a servant, but not subservient to your clients, and in turn by being a servant, you ultimately become the recipient. A huge recipient, as it turns out! Zig Ziglar says, "If you give others everything they want, you in turn will receive everything you want in return!" That statement has always had an impact on me, but the BY REFERRAL ONLY group harnessed this mindset into a powerful force!

> **A sidelight here: My young son, Brad was listening to some of my Zig Ziglar tapes, and was so impressed with Mr. Ziglar; he named his cat, "Ziggy"!**

So I packed up, and in early January, 1996 joined the BY REFERRAL ONLY group for the three day training in Dallas, Texas. This was held at The Grand Kempinski Hotel in Dallas. They called this training, The MAIN EVENT! At the time it lasted from 8AM to 8PM. There was an array of speakers going over the details of the BY REFERRAL ONLY program. I learned so much, my head was full, and aching. The program lasted for three twelve hour days, but the 36th hour was just as exciting and meaningful as was the first hour of the program. There was no let down in the enthusiasm and teachings from any of the BY REFERRAL ONLY program leaders. Joe Stumpf, bless his heart, I couldn't understand how he continued on for all these hours, and in fact to this day, I still don't know how he maintains such a high level of energy.

By the end of the first day, I knew that I wanted to join the "Coaching Club". It took until the end of the third day to actually complete the paperwork and make decision to commit the time and finances for the next year to learn and implement the systems.

I left Dallas with a 40 pound white box of tapes, manuals, information and hope!

I was hoping my wife would see the newfound enthusiasm from me, but not notice the large charge on the credit card! It worked, she never noticed the charge, and the credit card still had enough room on it for the payment! I knew I was on the way!

I called my processor, Rosanne, at home, and told her to wear blue jeans for the next three days; we were going to "blow up" our office! She was ready on Monday morning, and so was I. This was the start of a long, worthwhile and profitable journey with the BY REFERRAL ONLY organization.

That three day meeting in January 1996 **had as a profound** effect on my business life as did finding Jesus in a Baptist church in Beaumont Texas in February, 1973 did on my spiritual life! It was a meaningful event and allowed me to continue in the mortgage business with a childlike enthusiasm, and a rebirth for the business.

> **To say BY REFERRAL ONLY has been important to my business and personal life is a total and complete understatement!**

Arriving at the office on that fateful Monday morning after the MAIN EVENT, Rosanne didn't know what to expect. We sat down and reviewed what the MAIN EVENT entailed, and how it was going to change the business.

The main things I learned in that first MAIN EVENT was a complete mindset change. I learned to look at each and every contact with a client or prospect as a referral source. I learned that our closed clients were our most important business asset.

Roseanne and I began to establish a database of closed clients since Texas Supreme had opened in July 1993. I immediately began "mining the database" under the tutelage of Joe Stumpf and his band of coaches. I learned how to approach the clients, so that from the very first contact, they would start looking for referrals for me! Roseanne and I began implementing part of the BY REFERRAL ONLY process in a systematic step by step process.

It was not magic, and with the array of systems available from BY REFERRAL ONLY, it is easy for some people to go into "Overwhelm Mode", and get paralyzed with inertia. We didn't! We took one system, like a little squirrel with a nut. We took that system (nut), and worked it until it was in place, and then went to the next system. This was nothing fancy back then, and still isn't fancy today, but it works.

Fundamentals will work forever, if you work the fundamentals!

We began by starting our database of closed clients, writing a letter of apology to them for losing contact, and explaining that they would now be receiving monthly information from us—to be expecting it. I then began writing a series of letters to send to the families that currently had loans in process. We ended up sending seven letters to each family, updating them on the file in process, and of course asking for referrals. In fact, every time the phone rang, the first question I taught myself and my office girls, there were soon two, was to ask the caller, "Who Referred You To Us?"

I also implemented a monthly newsletter, what we call an "Evidence Of Success (EOS)". This EOS would describe the problem of a loan we had recently closed, tell how we solved the problem, and ask the client if they know someone just like this who could use our help. Of course, we never use names in these EOS letters so we don't embarrass anyone, or divulge their personal information. The EOS letters are one of the most important items I've extracted from BY REFERRAL ONLY over the many years I've been involved with them.

There is a specific writing format that is unique to BY REFERRAL ONLY, that drives the clients right back into your lap for repeat and referral business! This is not magic, but the results are magical when systematically performed with religious fervency.

We also implemented a series of conversations at application concerning referrals, and descriptions to help the clients remember us. One example would be explaining that in the next few weeks while they are going thru the lending process, they will notice more people than EVER before that need to get a loan for a refinance or a purchase. We call this the Reticular Activator. I use the example of them purchasing their favorite car. Asking what brand, model and color it is. Did you buy it new or used? So when you bought your new red Ford Thunderbird, did you see any other T-Birds on the road?
Almost everyone says emphatically yes, we see them everywhere now—all the T-Birds are red aren't they, they will ask? That's the Reticular Activator system kicking in; I never see red T-Birds, but White Montero Sports everywhere! The point I make with them is that just like the red T-Bird that's important to them, for the next few weeks getting your home loan will be one of the most important things going on in your life. You will notice more people than EVER before that need my services. "Will you refer them to me, if I do you a good job", I always ask? Of course no one says no, they LOVE you at application!

Our mindset was fully turning to becoming a true BY REFERRAL ONLY company!

I would participate regularly in the online phone calls from the dedicated coaches and Joe Stumpf himself. Each phone call brought more information and an increasing awareness of how important working my referral base was for current and future benefits. I learned from the staff and other participants from around the country. While a member of the coaching club, you are allowed to attend another MAIN EVENT of your choosing (or as many as you want) throughout the country.

I was like a man coming out of the desert. BY REFERRAL ONLY was the water, and I was soaking up and drinking as much as I could, as quickly as I could get the water! This knowledge from BY REFERRAL ONLY tasted so sweet, and furthermore, my business in 1996 started to explode! I was on a "water" high with new business! Ultimately, by December, 1996, my gross revenue had QUADRUPLED over 1995! Wow, was this a needed shot in the revenue arm!

Just like a man coming off the desert, the first "bucket" of water tasted so sweet, like never before. Then the fifth bucket of water still tasted good, but by the 10th bucket of water, the man from the desert feels he has had enough water to sustain him! I was like the man from the desert! I had drunk from the BY REFERRAL ONLY fountain until I thought I had enough to sustain me forever, because I had learned so much in that first year.

So at the end of 1996, even though my gross revenue had quadrupled, and my net income had risen astronomically, when my one year contract with BY REFERRAL ONLY was up, I didn't renew. Looking back, I think the main reason I ended up not renewing was that I failed to attend a second MAIN EVENT, and did not get immersed in the mindset for those three days again. Additionally, after a year of being successful, we get somewhat complacent. We got used to the information that is available, and took it for granted. Finally, deep down we think, "I can do this on my own, and save the BY REFERRAL ONLY fees!"

Was I wrong! I remember another story of Moses wandering in the desert for 40 years, before finding the Promised Land and being found. Well, it was only three years for me in the desert, I then found BY REFERRAL ONLY again! In November, 1999, I went to another MAIN EVENT, and rejoined the Coaching Club. It was an easy decision, and I did not have to hide the credit card receipt this time either!

During the three year absence, I can't say that the business suffered terribly. However we just drifted aimlessly. The systems we were religiously implementing and maintaining in 1996 while immersed in BY REFERRAL ONLY were adrift, and not as systematic. Even though the business did not suffer tremendously, we did not grow like we should have, or could have. So basically, we wasted three years!

Upon rejoining, I promised myself two things; 1) That I would go to at least two MAIN EVENTS annually, and 2) I would maintain active membership for a minimum of five years.

I have accomplished both of those items during the last five years. The business has once again grown, and is growing systematically.

In my three year absence, BY REFERRAL ONLY had changed dramatically by adding to its repertoire, yet the fundamentals were still the same. They were still advocating a high level of service, but not being subservient to our clients or real estate agents!

I still love that operational model!

Fundamentals will work forever, if you work the fundamentals!

Upon rejoining, I began to refresh myself with the old systems, and learning new systems, dialogs, and WOW—they had implemented a fantastic website! BY REFERRAL ONLY has literally a thousand points or systems or variations that can be implemented. The trick is to take a few systems and ideas that work for you, and work the system hard. More importantly, take baby steps—master one system at a time.

> **Before we go much farther in this chapter, let me point out something very important that you as a reader must know. I am a subscriber to, and an advocate for the BY REFERRAL ONLY system, and pay my annual dues like any other Coaching Club member!**
>
> **However, I am NOT a paid BY REFERRAL ONLY employee.**
>
> **Another point is there are many types of systems that you can use in your business or none at all. Several of these are noted in another chapter. It does not matter which system you work, IF you work the system. If you buy the system, and don't follow the parameters, don't blame the system for your lack of implementation.**
>
> **It's like a person reading a diet book while eating chocolate, and drinking a malted milk shake, and then proclaiming this diet book doesn't work—I'm still fat!!**
>
> **It's not the book, or system's fault, if you don't implement the system properly!**

OK, let's move on as Rascal Flatts sings in their song, "I'm Movin On"! And so am I!

Now that I've been back in BY REFERRAL ONLY for over five years, it's just ingrained into my work and life routine. The systems and dialogs learned, and adapted over this period have added to the stability of my business. Obviously, there are always intermittent downturns or cyclical outside influences that will affect this and any business. In the long run though, by systemizing your business, it will continue to support you and grow as much as you want it to grow.

My goal has always been to have a life and a work life!

Let's repeat that, yes, "My goal has always been to have a life and a work life!" Since joining BY REFERRAL ONLY, I've learned that we don't have to be 24/7 mortgage or real estate professionals. By systemizing your business, you can turn on or off the spigot of incoming clients and work flow. The system will give you the confidence that the business is out there, you just have to "mine it"! Think of your database as a giant goldmine. **You** decide how deep you want to mine the "ore" out of the goldmine.

So that my life and work life could have as much stability as possible, I decided to implement several systems so that my clients could depend on us, and we could depend on the system!

In November, 1999, I dedicated myself to systematically mailing my EOS cards out monthly for 5 years without missing a month. These cards would go out on the 15th of each month with a standard color, and give the "story" of a loan closed in the prior month or two. I have done this each month!

I also dedicated myself to attending two MAIN EVENTS somewhere each year. These three day events are held monthly somewhere in the US or Canada. I have completed this task on average each year, attending 11 MAIN EVENTS in 5 years! By attending these events, I have met some wonderful and productive agents in from across America. In fact, for the last three years, I've received enough referrals from other Coaching Club members to pay for the Coaching Club!

At these MAIN EVENTS several things are occurring; 1) We are being immersed in the BY REFERRAL ONLY techniques and strategies, 2) There are people from all over the country attending, so we are learning on an informal setting at lunch and in the evening what other like minded professionals are doing to stay productive, 3) We are having fun, and meeting real estate agents and lenders, some highly successful, and some just getting started in their professional life. I come home ready to set the world on fire, again!

I also dedicated myself to learning and then adapting the BY REFERRAL ONLY dialogues in engaging the clients, and preparing them to give you referrals forever! These dialogues help us to pinpoint the client's needs and responsibilities of working with a "BY REFERRAL ONLY" mortgage professional.

I also wanted to know as much as possible about the new BY REFERRAL ONLY website. This website was so helpful and enlightening, and by itself would have been worth the price of the Coaching Club. I generally would spend 30-40 minutes daily just "wandering" around the website. I have been learning and examining what other lenders and real estate pros were using for marketing and what other ideas were working well in their businesses.

We also have a monthly *"Results In Action"* kit that has several important pieces of information, and a current CD interviewing one of the top lenders or agents in the country. The kit also has several ready to use letters and strategies. Download and Go!
I read this journal as soon as the package is opened, and pop in the CD to learn additional information from another top professional from around the country!

Each Trimester, BY REFERRAL ONLY also produces a very professional journal (the *Results In Action* magazine) and invites all members and their assistants to attend a regional Community Remodel Day for a day of enlightenment. These are beneficial for recharging the batteries between MAIN EVENTS. I seldom miss these CRD meetings.

BY REFERRAL ONLY also has a series of coaches that are available to each member. These coaches are available by phone, fax, email, and I imagine smoke signal too, if needed. Jen Brown, Sarah Ace and Shawn Harris have helped me immensely during the last five years. More about the coaches later!

Another aspect of BY REFERRAL ONLY that is very important, are the teleconferences that are held daily. There must be 30-40 different calls you could participate in if so desired each month. The array of TeleClasses is amazing. There are classes on New Member Orientation, Basic Foundation Principles, Time and Planning seminars, Web Clinics, Marketing, Assistants Training, Hotline Training, and others by Joe Stumpf and other top executives in the BY REFERRAL ONLY organization.

If you miss the actual live TeleClass, within a few days you are able to go to the website and listen to the TeleClass at your leisure. This is an invaluable tool since many times our schedules will not allow us to be in two places at once.

Finally, BY REFERRAL ONLY produces another event twice annually where attendees learn to be the best managers in the world thru the Strategic Leader Meetings. I have not personally attended this meeting, but will soon.
Below is an excerpt from the website describing the event!

Strategic Leader is a bi-annual program open to all active members interested in "growing" their business to work with them - or without them. Topics focus specifically on building strong, profitable teams through key areas of structure, hiring, training and compensation. Each Strategic Leader Program highlights a different topic related to growing your business.

As can be imagined, BY REFERRAL ONLY will give you every opportunity to succeed if you just work the system! These are fundamental systems.

Fundamentals will work forever, if you work the fundamentals!

What I outlined was the basic BY REFERRAL ONLY opportunities within their events and curriculum. The proof is in the details and results. After being a member since 1996, I can attest that the system works, if you work the system!

The System Works, If You Work The System!

Looking way back, it's hard to remember not being in the BY REFERRAL ONLY community. The best analogy I can think of is comparing the feeling to having your first child. Prior to being parents, everyone said, "That new baby will change your life"! But, did you believe it--Not Really--How much could a little baby affect you life?   Reality set in upon arriving home from the hospital with our first young son Brian, and within two months, we could not remember ever NOT having a baby! This is similar to the BY REFERRAL ONLY system. Once you are immersed in the program, it's hard to remember never being a member!

Five years after rejoining BY REFERRAL ONLY, my systems are well established. Some were easy to implement, and others, along with specific wording and dialogs came slowly to me. My coaches had to keep reminding me that the programs would work, if I would work the program and system.   Sounds familiar?

Let me give you a few of examples, and the results. I ultimately combined the three systems listed below into a newsletter with phenomenal results. More about that later!

Letter From The Heart

I was, and still am, just learning about what is called, "The Letter From The Heart"! The concept here is that you open up to your database in a newsletter a little bit each month recounting some aspect of the events in your life. Reasoning, that as people know more about you and can relate to you, they will also refer more of their friends and family.

The "Letter From The Heart" is only written to people in your database that already know you, love you and trust you. This is not written, in my opinion, to a farm area or to unsolicited databases.   They would not know you, and the letter would have little or no impact.

I understood the principle, and could see the reasoning behind the letter, but I was scared! Scared, yes scared of rejection, scared of not being able to write effectively, just scared!
I kept telling my coach, "you don't understand, I'm a big ol' fat Texas boy, this sounds like some of that *California avocado stuff*!" She laughed, and kept telling me, "Wes, just try it and see what happens. Test it once"!

Finally, I did. My mother had recently died, and I wrote my first "Letter From The Heart!"

WOW, I could not believe what happened! (A copy of the letter is below!)

My phone started ringing off the hook from clients calling to give their sympathy.
15 sympathy cards arrived. Everyone was supportive of this big ol fat Texas boy!

The most unusual call came from a car salesman, whom I had bought a car from about a year earlier. He told me he had asked his sales manager if he could read this letter from a client of his. So he starts to read my letter to the dozen car salesmen. Now remember, some of these people are similar to "hardened criminals". Not really, but they *are* car salesmen! So he reads the letter, and looks up as he was finishing. Four of the salesmen had left to go make phone calls, four more had tears in their eyes, and the sales manager disbanded the meeting. This letter really made an impact on them and others.

One of the tenants of BY REFERRAL ONLY is to write to make an impact on the recipient.

Time Is Short!!

Please support me while I write this to you.

My Mother recently died. This has been a very sad time, but Mom lived until she died. What I mean is that she enjoyed life daily, not waiting until the <u>perfect</u> time to have "fun". In fact, she was Line Dancing just the day before she died of a heart attack quietly in her sleep at her home. She was 77 years old and planning a trip to New York City with her senior friends. At her funeral, all of her friends said she was the life of the party and would be missed. I don't doubt it!

In the last three years, she and I had become much closer in our relationship than in the last 30 years. We really enjoyed each others company for the past three years. It was hard to believe how time passed so quickly!

I am so thankful we were able to reunite; it is never too late to reconnect.

As we enter this holiday season, please don't wait 30 years like I did to reconnect with someone you love, since time is short. If there is someone whom you have wanted to pick up the phone or write a note to and say, "hello", "I love you", or "I'm sorry", DO IT NOW!

Time Is Short!

Thanks for listening.

Wes Cordeau
"The Dreammaker"

I think it worked, especially for my first, "Letter From The Heart!" I was scared no more!

Again, the primary purpose is to have the client know a little more about you and your family each month. The writings "open" you up to your database of people that already know you, love you and trust you like a flower. This flower is opening like a spring bouquet!

The concept in writing the Letter from The Heart, is to write it as if you are writing to one person only. This is an excellent example of the Letter from The Heart!

Since this first "Letter From The Heart", I have written dozens of others with varying degrees of impact. Topics have been as varied as is available to almost any family. Some of the topics have been:

- Anatomy of buying a new car
- Thoughts on sending our first child off to college
- Thoughts on sending our last child off to college, and the empty nest
- Announcing, and thoughts on finding out I had Diabetes
- Letter concerning accepting our new daughter-in-law into our family
- Several Christmas letters, concerning giving and helping others
- Several have been on travel, and our vacation trips around the USA
- How it felt to turn (a young) 50
- A letter regarding our oldest son completing college and entering the workforce
- Thoughts on our home of 20+ years being flooded in Tropical Storm Allison
- A story concerning how "frazzled" people get in traffic
- Thoughts on a good friend dying young
- Several positive thinking articles on living, and being alive in America
- The details of our youngest son's teenage problems, and its effect on us

From this short list, you'll notice there is an array of topics. Some were very meaningful, and had a huge impact on several individuals. All articles were written with compassion.

> When I wrote the details on our young son's "growing" pains as a teenager, I had two mothers call in tears thanking me for writing about our trials and tribulations. They were going thru the exact same turmoil with their child now. The mothers thought they were alone, and were the only family to have ever experienced this situation.

The "Letter from The Heart" is an important tool to use for your database!

Each "Letter From The Heart" is written using the FORD strategy! The FORD strategy is an excellent discussion template for engaging people in conversation. Follow this formula, and everyone will think you are a genius, and the best conversationalist in the whole universe!

F   Family
O   Occupation
R   Recreation
D   Dreams

All "Letters from the Heart" are built on the FORD strategy. If you build your discussion with clients, or anyone new that you meet around the FORD principle, and you listen to them describe their Family, Occupation, Recreation and Dreams, they will think YOU are the smartest person around.

On the other hand, leave PRS, until later! PRS is short for:

P	**Politics**
R	**Religion**
S	**Sex**

The PRS subjects are to be avoided at almost all costs.

The ultimate result of the "Letter From The Heart" to me has been that my clients now rely on me as a friend, confidant and consultant in areas far removed from just "mortgages" or "the mortgage man"!

If someone will consult with you on where to send their daughter to college, they certainly will let you refinance their home, and not moan and groan if you are a quarter rate point higher than "low cost, no cost mortgage" advertised in Sunday's paper!

Evidence Of Success

The purpose of the Evidence of Success (EOS) is to take a loan and break it down into the following components:

1) Describe what was difficult about the loan
2) Tell how you were able to solve the client's problem
3) Indicate how you will be able to solve other problems just like this one
4) Ask for more loans like this one

Very simple yet effective! As mortgage professionals, we know that every loan has some challenges. Most of the time, we just go about our daily business solving very complex issues, and then go on to the next complex issue!

By using the EOS format, we now can turn a pure financial transaction into a relationship model. When writing the EOS, and putting the loan into words that the general public understands, we become much more referable because the loan is not "just a loan", but a lesson in problem solving.
Most clients don't actually need a mortgage loan, they need their problems solved!

That's why my clients labeled me "The Dreammaker"!
(An EOS example is included later.)

Let's look at the language of a real estate transaction:

In each transaction, there are two parts: 1) Building the Relationship, which develops the transaction on a personal, emotional level (the Heart), and, 2) Transactional, which develops the transaction on an analytical level (the Head).

The language of the Heart which is most associated with real estate agents, and sounds like this; "Oh Mr. Smith, you could cook some gourmet meals from this fabulous kitchen", " Mrs. Smith, wouldn't your children just love this swimming pool with the waterfall and sliding board", or "Look at this romantic fireplace in this oversized master bedroom"! You get the picture—all "flowery" wording, that helps to cement the "Heart" relationship between the client and the real estate agent!

Now, let's look at the language most associated with the mortgage professionals; "Mr. Smith, it seems you have more debt than needed", "Mrs. Smith, could you explain the late payment 2 years ago on your MasterCard?", "Mr. Smith, it appears that your ratios are a little high for the home that you and your wife picked out for your family", "I know the real estate agent said your payment would be $1,492 monthly, but she failed to include the Mortgage Insurance, Home Owners Association Fees and Flood Insurance that we have to count in the ratios". You can easily see the difference in language. The mortgage professional's language is detailed, analytical, precise, hard and if smart, under promising! The mortgage language is most associated with the "Head".

It is easy to see why most real estate agents are invited to the barbeques--not the mortgage professionals! It is also easy to see why most mortgage professionals tend to over promise and under deliver. We want to please the client, but in pleasing the client we also must deliver a complete loan package to the processor and ultimately to the lender.

If you tell the "Smiths" that they will close their loan in 30 days at a 5.25%, 30 year fixed mortgage, and move in for $5,900, and you meet EVERY one of the parameters, you have simply done your job! That's what you get paid for--Right? The transactions over, you did your job, you got paid handsomely (hopefully), and now you're on to the next family! If you leave it at that stopping point, the Smiths have no real reason to refer friends, family and co-workers to you. In fact, they really don't realize what you did behind the scenes to get their loan completed on target and at the rate promised at application.

Let's help them remember how complex of a loan it was thru the EOS format! Again, the EOS is written as if you are writing to one person only, just like "The Letter From The Heart!" Below is an example of an EOS!

I Didn't Know They Could Do That?

Just a quick note to let you know how we helped someone and can do the same for you or someone you refer to us!! This is a continuing series of successes from Wes Cordeau.

A few months back, I met a new Doctor in residency. Going from almost no income to a substantial income is quite an accomplishment; however, he still had almost no cash to work with right now. However, he was going to have a big tax problem at year end because of his newfound income!! Ummmm--what to do????

I knew we could find and fund his loan; we have over 500 products to offer. We put together a 100% purchase program, with the seller paying most of his closing costs. Just to be sure, we went ahead and had him pre-approved before the house hunting began so there would be little or no questions later! He is now a happy homeowner!! 8-}}

We also discussed life challenges in investing, savings, and other such mundane items as in paying off his home early and building a substantial net worth. Although he is a sharp cookie in the medical field, most doctors are dunces in the financial field.

Finally, this 100% program works for all types of professionals just coming to the job market, and earning a substantial income, not just doctors, lawyers or Indian Chiefs!!

PS: If you know of someone that needs expert mortgage advice for 100% financing, please call me with their phone number.

Wes Cordeau 281-445-1901   Cell: 713-899-0091

This is an excellent example of setting up the problem, solving it, and asking for other loans just like this one!

Referral Corner

Each month, I include in my newsletter, a section I call "Referral Corner"! In this section, I thank each person for the act of referring clients, regardless of the outcome.
Their responsibility is to send the referral to me; I'll live with the outcome. Some months, almost all of the referrals turn into transactions, and some months they do not. I know that in the long-term, if my data base of closed clients keeps sending referrals, my life will be OK!

The Referral Corner establishes what I like to call "Social Proof"! Social Proof indicates that if 15-20 people are being referred to me each month, we must be doing something right, so it's acceptable to send additional referrals. Similar to your mother asking when you were young, "If Johnny is jumping off a bridge, will you do it too?" Well, in this case we want everyone to continue "jumping", as in referring their family friends and coworkers to us for new mortgage loans! I have a sample "Referral Corner" below for you review!

Thanks For Your Referrals--Last Month,
They are the lifeblood of our business.
Who is the next person you know that is most likely to
Borrow for a Home Purchase or Refinance?

A referral is when you send someone you care about, to someone you trust and respect!
These are the people who respected us enough to send people they care about to us!

Karen Randle	Molly Cordeau	James Kuehn
David Host	Barbara Caldwell	William West
Cindy Usai	Heather Walters	Gus Hernandez
Ted Mayeux	Ed Loesch	Frank Edwards
Jeff Neal		

(Your Name Here Next Month)

Again, like the "Letter From The Heart", and EOS, we thank people as if they are the only one we are thanking!

This led to an interesting phone call.

Once, I had a man call me and tell me, "Wes, I don't want you to include my name in the newsletter next month"!   Ok, I replied, but "Billy Bob", I don't have recorded anyone that you referred this month. Did you refer anyone to me this month, Billy Bob? No, but it says right here, that **"Your Name Here Next Month",** he replied. I see; he took it literally that I was going to include his name there next month, since he FELT LIKE he was the only one receiving a copy of the newsletter.   **Mission Accomplished!**

In the Chapter, Database Mining For Fun and Profits, I have included several examples of the entire "newsletter"!

What you are reading here is a few broad points learned and adapted through the BY REFERRAL ONLY systems and strategies. Many other things they have taught me have become integrated into my system and life.

Remember, we want to have a life and a work life!

Other Things Learned From BY REFERRAL ONLY

There are literally hundreds of other tidbits of information learned over the years, but some of the most important items are the simplest and most productive.

1) I learned a dialogue to ask new clients that were referred to me that is so effective in cementing our new relationship, based on the relationship of the "old client", and the new client to me, I can't believe I resisted my coaches' suggestions for 6 months.
This simple question will cement the new relationship!

2) I learned a series of dialogues, and questions that easily explains the complete BY REFERRAL ONLY process to new clients. This 10 step formula is priceless.

3) I learned the importance of consistent communication with current and former clients.

4) I learned how useful the information on the BY REFERRAL ONLY website is, so that we don't have to reinvent the wheel each time a problem or opportunity arises.

5) I learned that other professionals across the country could be useful sources of information and referrals, and vice versa. Everyone I've encountered associated with BY REFERRAL ONLY has been first class in their attitude!

In summary; BY REFERRAL ONLY has been a Godsend to me since 1996. I only wished that I had known about them earlier in my career. There is so much to learn about business, marketing and living a fulfilled life that can be short circuited by relying on something else other than just yourself, and your small sphere of influence. The people I've encountered thru BY REFERRAL ONLY from Joe Stumpf, to the receptionist have one thing in common;

To help you have the best life ever, and the best work life you wish to have!

To access the BY REFERRAL ONLY website, please go to:

www.ByReferralOnly.com

At this website, even as a visitor, there is a huge amount of valuable information to be learned and a 45 minute business building workshop for free. Go to "Free Tools"!
You can also sign up for Free Marketing Nuggets that will be emailed to you twice monthly. You might be thinking, with all this free stuff—Why would I go to the MAIN EVENT or join the Coaching Club? Good Question!

It goes back to the basic philosophy of BY REFERRAL ONLY, which states that you lead with the giving hand to reap the rewards later and forever!

The BY REFERRAL ONLY website says it best:

Why? It's quite simply our way of introducing you to the depth and breath of the business-building strategies available to you at BY REFERRAL ONLY. It's a business-building strategy that we believe and teach, called "Leading With The Giving Hand." **Simply put, when you give freely with no strings attached, you receive tenfold.**

This offer is available to you right now just by calling 800-950-7325, Extension #2. Please take us up on it. We're here to serve you.

Onward we go, learning more how to be a highly paid professional mortgage loan officer!

**If you have an interest in joining this dynamic team, call 281-445-1901, X204 for the "President's Hotline"
or
Email: Wes@TexasSupremeMortgage.com**

DataBase Mining!

How To Turn Your DataBase Into Gold!

You might not be aware of the gold mine you are sitting on in your closed files. By "mining" these files you can turn useless paper into gold. This is a process that starts long before closing occurs. If you wait until closing to start "cashing" in on referrals, you are way too late!

Initial Contact!

We actually start mining our database at the first contact with any prospect. When the phone rings, we will ask them first; **"Who referred you to us?"** This sets up the expectation that all borrowers are referred to us, OR they will refer all their friends, family and co-workers to us for future transactions. Each contact from that moment until the end of the relationship is built on referrals. They trusted us enough to get them into their dream home, they should know us, love us and trust us enough with every person they know, unless WE do something to break that trust!

Application!

At application, we again discuss referrals in detail, and the fact that our business is built on referrals as suggested by the BY REFERRAL ONLY strategies. One question of many that I've used for several years seems to pinpoint and solidify the referral process.
I'll ask the borrower at application a series of direct questions. I'll ask the borrower about the "referrer"; "Mary" is the referring prior client.

Me: "Mary referred you to me. How do you know Mary?"
Borr: "I know Mary from work"
Me: "Do you generally trust Mary?"
Borr: "Sure, I trust Mary"
(If they didn't trust Mary, the borrower wouldn't be here in the first place)
Me: "So let me ask you, What did Mary tell you about me?"
Borr: "Oh, Mary said you were great, and friendly, and ….."
Me: "Really, wow, Mary said some nice things about me."
Me: "What else did she say?"
Borr: "Umm well, she said you would tell us the truth—sometimes the brutal truth"
Me: "Interesting, Mary really said some nice things about me. I'll tell you what, I promise to try to live up to each one of those statements throughout the loan process. Fair enough?
Borr: "Fair enough"
Me: "One final thought before we plunge into the loan process. If I do you a good job on your mortgage loan, a good job being I'm friendly, truthful and deliver you a mortgage you can live with—will you refer all your friends, family and co-workers—just like Mary does?"

Borr: "Sure—of course I will"
(Remember from a previous chapter—at application the borrower always loves you the most---they will agree to almost anything)
Me: "Because, truly, we are working for two people or families in this transaction;
We are working for you to get you your mortgage and home, but we are also working for Mary because she is a great referral source, and we don't want to lose Mary's future referrals either! Who says you can't serve two masters!"

I've found that this dialogue sets the stage for future referrals from the current borrower. Let me point out that my California Coach from BY REFFERAL ONLY worked on me for six months to try this wording before actually using the above words. Once, I used those statements with the borrowers—WOW—I couldn't believe how good I felt when the borrowers were saying all those nice things about me! Cool Eh!

I also couldn't believe how resistant I was to trying something so beneficial!

There are many other areas concerning referrals that are used at application to set the "mood" for future referrals, but I've found this dialogue to be the most productive.

Think how easy this is to deliver to the borrower! All we have to do is be friendly, tell the truth and deliver a mortgage loan for their new home, and they'll refer their friends, family and co-workers to us forever. Sounds like a good tradeoff to me!

Other BY REFERRAL ONLY members get much more detailed than I do, but this process works well for me at application.

Processing a Loan!

When a loan is in process is a very important time to continue setting the stage for future referrals. Some brokers get many referrals during this stage—however we don't. But, we do set the stage to hit a home run after the loan closes. For us, it seems like once the loan is closed, a flood of referrals from the new homeowners come to us. So this stage is very important.

We send out a simple set of letters addressing different issues during the course of the loan that helps the borrower remember their commitment to us concerning referrals. The letters we send are as follows:
1) TIL explanation with a paragraph concerning referrals.
2) Welcome letter from the processor, welcoming them to the TSMI family, and a paragraph concerning referrals.
3) A "Hassle Free" referral card; asking for referrals.
4) Mid-term report—We update the borrower on the loan; and ask for referrals.
5) Appraisal Pictures and Floor Plan; We notice at closing when explaining the appraisal to the borrowers that they pay most attention to the pictures and home floor plan. So we send these to the borrowers early with a letter that says, "start arranging your furniture

and showing your friends your new home you're trying to purchase." (This wording is subject to the status of the loan)

6) Thank You letter—asking for referrals.
7) Amortization letter-asking for referrals.

Each contact point, whether in person, telephone, snail mail or email speaks to the importance of referrals? **Referrals are the lifeblood of our business!**

Approval Notification!

Generally, when we get a loan approval—we are so happy—we just call the client and tell them they're approved. As I heard someone describe it—just "vomit" out the results! Right? Wrong!! You have to **stage the approval** notification so that the client appreciates what we have done for them during the loan process. You must take the borrower behind the scenes letting them know how hard you fought for their loan approval, so that they will appreciate you. This appreciation will translate into many future loan referrals.

If we simply call up the client and tell them they are approved, we have lost the referral moment. In general, when calling the client to tell them of the approval, you want to describe the process before telling them the results.

It may sound like this:
Me: "Hello, Bob, Wes here"
Bob: "Hi Wes, How's it going?"
Me: "Bob, I'm calling about your loan"
Bob: "Yes, did we get it, is everything OK?"
Me: "Bob, remember at application I was a little concerned about your bonus income, and also about the appraisal—since you have only owned the home for 2 years, and we needed quite a bit more value than when you purchased the home?"
Bob: "Yes, Wes, is everything OK?"
Me: "Bob, I told you I'd do the best I could to get the loan approved, and I have tried"
Bob: "Oh no, Wes!"
Me: "Bob, I sent the loan to our favorite lender, and they liked the home, but the bonus income is bothersome", So, I sent it to a backup lender and they were OK with the bonus income, but felt the home wasn't worth the increase in value over the last two years"
Bob: "Oh no, Wes thanks for working so hard to help us"
Me: "Finally, my processor said—Bob's going to get approved somehow—let's go to this third lender"
Me: "Guess what Bob, the third time really was the charm. They approved you for the refinance, and we were able to keep the rate as we thought we could at application"
Bob: "Thanks Wes—you really had me worried"
Me: "Bob, I went the extra mile to get this loan approved for you.
        Was this important to you?"
Bob: "Of course, it was extremely important Wes"

Me: "Bob, Who is the next person you know that needs a little extra service from us?"

Now, do you get the picture? There's actually a lot more to this process, but this scenario gives a flavor of the dialogue when you are setting up a "referral moment". The borrower will respect you much more than simply calling and saying "Your loan is approved-- Congratulations!"

Most lenders and loan officers fail miserably at this juncture.

Alternate Approval Notification!

We also have another alternative system that we use on approvals, instead of the phone call. This process works extremely well under the right circumstances. It works best for office workers, and if there are not too many outstanding conditions on the loan.

In this process, we will send a little ice cooler with Texas Supreme Mortgage name on the side, filled with sodas, peanuts and "non-melting" candy to the borrower's office. We do not put ice in the cooler (or alcohol) for the delivery due to concerns of leakage. We'll get a helium filled "Congratulations" balloon, and have it delivered. We have streamers with our business cards attached. Everyone knows what happens with a delivery like this to their office. A crowd gathers, everyone wants to know who sent the package to Mary! The excitement builds! Mary opens the attached letter of Loan Approval! Eureka!!

It's now like the Happiest Place On Earth!!

Her co-workers all grumble, "My Loan Officer didn't do that for me, they just called and said we were approved!" Mary's loan officer is obviously different from the rest!

I've had people call obviously munching on peanuts or cookies and sounding like they were at a party sponsored by TSMI!! The total cost on this referral moment is under $30.
The benefits are tremendous. When people are recognized in public, they think better of you, because you were thoughtful enough to do this for them! Not to them!

Some of these scenarios may seem a little corny or childish, but when you see the results, you will forget about being a little corny or childish!

In fact, we all should have a little more childlike enthusiasm in our lives!

Closing!

Or as they like to call it in BY REFERRAL ONLY, the Celebration! This is another easy referral moment. Just by attending closing with the borrower, you are already in the vast minority. When I look around at other closings, I seldom ever see another mortgage loan officer attending. In fact, if it's a real estate agent or escrow officer I know, I'll stick my head in the door and chide them—"Where's your loan officer on this transaction? If you need anything explained, I'll be right next door."

We are doing the family a disservice by not attending the closing if at all possible. These are our numbers making up the transaction. We are an integral part of the transaction. In fact, without a mortgage, there is NO transaction. The most important aspect though, is this may be the last time we see the borrower in person forever, or until their next transaction. This is an excellent time to solidify the relationship by being there at a critical time in the process—The Closing!

At a **purchase closing**, I like to take the purchasers aside with the HUD1 Settlement Statement and explain the details line by line. I take them by themselves, without the real estate agent. In this separate room, I explain who the players will be in the conference room. In a perfect world, the purchaser would have received all documents and the settlement statement two days before closing to review and inspect them; however, rarely is it a perfect world.

The reason we are discussing the settlement statement privately is to insure they can ask me any questions without the fear of looking "silly" in the conference room with the sellers, the agents and the escrow officer. We then go to the conference room, and sometimes the closer will explain again, and sometimes we will begin signing. It is up to the purchaser and closer. People appreciate not being put in an uncomfortable situation.

Once the paperwork is signed and the closer is faxing papers to the lender for release of the funds, I take the appraisal and go over it in detail with the borrowers. At this point, I also take three pictures of the purchasers and their agent. I send one to the agent, one to the purchaser and one is put in our application room for others to see a picture of a "happy homeowner."

Generally, I'll also take a picture or two of the seller and their agent, and send them a copy after closing too. No one gets left out of the pictures! I'll send these pictures along with a thank you note, and of course asking for referrals along with the pictures. Finally, I've had two different high-end digital cameras, and found them to be more trouble than my trusty old 35MM and just take the film to Walgreen's for printing. It saves me time, effort and AGGRAVATION to simplify the process. I'm quite sure it's an operator malfunction, and not the digital cameras! Do whatever you are comfortable with, but just be sure to complete this task. It is worth the effort!

At a **refinance closing,** the situation is changed because there is no seller or agents involved. Generally, I'll just have the escrow closer explain the HUD1 settlement statement. If it is a repeat borrower, I may not take new pictures, but on a new refinance, I will be sure to get their photos for the wall!

Seldom will I leave closing without at least one name from someone for a referral.

> If this seems like too much work and effort to begin and maintain a relationship, just think how much work and effort it is to be broke, dissatisfied, and unsuccessful?
> Or, you could run another ad in the local real estate magazine like everybody else, or buy some mortgage leads and "hope" for some new business to come to you!
> Where would you rather spend your time?

Post Closing Followup!

In BY REFERRAL ONLY, we call this, the "After" division!

We have come this far just to get to closing, and to include the new borrower's information into our database. The previous information in this chapter is a setup for the final steps in "mining" our database of closed files! Now the fun and profit really begins.

There are many different database management systems you can use; Mark-it Systems; Act; GoldMine and TopProducer are just a few of the more popular systems available. You can easily design your own system, based on your individual needs and desires as to how you actually strata the file. We have a very simple system, but it works for us!

The individual system is not as important as the concept of setting up some type of database management system. The key is to set up the system after the FIRST closing.
The next most important function is to follow up on a regular consistent basis with meaningful information.

I use a very simple "newsletter" to communicate monthly with my entire database of closed clients, and then quarterly I send "something" to a special group of top referrers.
To my special group, I'll send some note pads, a letter opener, bookmarks, magnetic sports schedules or something that has "life", not to be easily discarded!

In The Chapter on BY REFERRAL ONLY, I described the pieces of this newsletter.
I've chosen to completely write and manage this process in-house. There are thousands of commercial newsletters you can subscribe to that are probably OK. However, I want my monthly information to the clients to have an impact, and they know that it is from me. It takes me **less than an hour monthly** to write, format and have newsletter printed.
We have outsourced the final details of labels, stamping and mailing. Either way is ok.

The key is consistent meaningful communication with your database!

I might think my writing style is brilliant, witty and charming, but the most important piece of the puzzle is to get the newsletter out at the same time monthly, using the same color combination and with a consistent message to the recipients.

That's it, that's the secret to mining your database! However, there are some more details that you might want to know.

Let's recap what the newsletter components look like and why they are important:

1. I use 67# Yellow Cardstock from Office Depot, 8 ½" x 11", folded in half.
2. This will make four "sides" for information.
3. Side 1—Label
4. Side 2—Letter From The Heart; FORD Strategy
5. Side 3—Referral Corner; Thank the referrers monthly
6. Side 4—Evidence Of Success; Describe a successful loan
7. Mail at the same day-15th—of each month; rain or shine

I have included some examples of the entire newsletter; you'll notice there are no recipes from Aunt Tillie or current events. There are just my personal writings. Either way you go, a commercial or homespun newsletter is not wrong, just get it mailed consistently to the people that know you, love you and trust you already from prior closings to begin mining your database!

Texas Supreme Mortgage, Inc.
505 N. Sam Houston Pkwy., E., Ste 110
Houston, Texas 77060

Drop me an email @
wcordeau@aol.com

"By Referral Only"
Your "Mortgage Consultant" For Life
  281-445-1901

Side 1—Label Side

Print, place a label, stamp it and you are ready to mail the newsletter!

We use a very simple database management system from Microsoft Windows, and print out the labels for this side. Others I know do a mail merge and actually print the label information on this side. Either way works, "Just Do It"!

Do It Now!! There Is No Perfect Time!!

I was listening to a friend of mine trying to convince himself that there would be a better time to start raising a family. This got me thinking, that there is seldom a perfect time, place or setting for anything. We simply deal with the challenges as they arrive.

If we waited for just the right time to start a family, change careers, move to another city, even break up a family, we would most likely just prolong the inevitable. Waiting for the perfect time plays right into the hands of procrastination!!

Then while we procrastinate, the situation grows larger and more ominous in our head, like mold growing in a dark, dank room of our mind!!   So what is the solution??

Get all the facts together, sort out the facts and emotional aspects of the decision, evaluate the short and long term repercussions of the decision and THEN DECIDE!! There is a management theory that goes like this: Ready, Aim, Fire, Aim, Aim, Aim, Aim!! Meaning that after the decision is made, pick your target, go towards the target and adjust as you go near the target, and eventually you will hit the target!!

Once the decision is made, put 100% effort into supporting the outcome!!

Take care until next month!!

Side 2-Letter From The Heart
Letter from the Heart is always written using the FORD strategy!

Thanks For Your Referrals--Last Month,
They are the lifeblood of our business.
Who is the next person you know that is most likely to
Borrow for a Home Purchase or Refinance?

A referral is when you send someone you care about, to someone you trust and respect! These are the people who respected us enough to send people they care about to us!

Karen Randle	Christine Pell	Suzette Kirchner
Ruben Villarreal, Sr.	Ed Woodruff	Stan Kuper
Matt Haidenyak	Ruben Villarreal Jr	Sheila Childers
James Kuehn	John Rucinsky	Cherion Cherion
Jose Bucio	Laura Rucinsky	Summer Adams
Tom Wier	Randy Hon	Jacalyn Henthorne

(Your Name Here Next Month)

Side 3—Referral Corner

The Referral Corner is "social proof", that if others are referring their friends, family and co-workers to us, we must be treating them with care! Obviously, we do treat them with care. The subliminal message is **(Your Name Here Next Month)!** Send Wes a referral and your name will be in print also!

It Took Two Years To Get Rid Of My Brother

Just a quick note to let you know how we helped someone and can do the same for you or someone you refer to us!! This is a continuing series of successes from Wes Cordeau.

We recently closed a transaction for a client that had gone thru a nasty divorce (like almost all of them) and was bunking with his brother and his family. Unfortunately he had been living there two years and had not saved much cash since he was cleaning up after the divorce.

Fortunately, his credit was in pretty respectable shape.

He was referred by his brother (WES--get him outta my house--quick--he says!), and once we analyzed his financial situation, we felt like we could get him into a home. There were several ZERO down options available, with the seller paying much of the closing costs too!! We ended up getting him pre-approved, even before finding a home.

With the pre-approval in hand, now all he did with his Realtor was find a home, structure the deal and NOW, he is a happy homeowner--actually, we now have two happy homeowners!! ::)))

PS: If you know of someone that wants to purchase a home with not much cash, please call me with their phone number. **Wes Cordeau 281-445-1901**

Side 4—Evidence Of Success

In the EOS, we describe the problem, tell how we solved it, and ask for more loans like this one described and solved!

XXXXXXXXXXXXXXXXXXXXXXXXXXXXXXXXXXXXXXXXXXXXXXXXXXX

Repeat month after month after month after month!

Texas Supreme Mortgage, Inc.
505 N. Sam Houston Pkwy., E., Ste 110
Houston, Texas 77060

Remember, we have money to lend!

"By Referral Only"
Your "Mortgage Consultant" For Life
 281-445-1901

Side 1—Label Side

100 Things I Want To Do Before I Die!!

Have you ever really thought about it? I was at a seminar last year and we were asked to come up with 100 things to do before dying!! WELL, I could only come up with about 7 right off the bat.
I kept working at it for about two weeks and amazingly, was able to identify these 100 things.

The 100 items usually center on the FORD principal.
F-family; O-occupation; R-recreation; D-dreams

There are some standard ones, like being a billionaire, looking like Fabio, and going to the moon!! Then there are some outlandish ones, like reading the Bible from cover to cover, traveling around the world in 80 days and playing the top 100 golf courses in the world.
Might be able to do all of those together in one grand world tour!!

Finally, I decided that our two boys and my wife could come up with their own list and we could cross-check our lists. The boys (Brian & Brad) were not amused or enthused about this project!
Ya know the saying, "Money Talks", well it does at our house.
After offering each son a $1.00 for each item on the list (up to a $100.00), they were ready to get started. WOW---if you ever want to know what's going on in your kids head, try this!!

Many items were pretty standard, but then, I was amazed at the thought provoking items that each one came up with, such as: helping the poor in Africa for 30 days, teaching their own kid to play ball, helping with homework, and many more service type functions.
It truly brought tears to my eyes!!   Try it, you may be amazed!!
LET ME KNOW HOW THIS TURNS OUT

Side 2—Letter from The Heart

**Thanks For Your Referrals--Last Month,
They are the lifeblood of our business.
Who is the next person you know that is most likely to
Borrow for a Home Purchase or Refinance?**

**A referral is when you send someone you care about, to someone you trust and
respect!
These are the people who respected us enough to send people they care about to us!**

Karen Randle	Gene & Adela Rogers	Suzette Kirchner
Ruben Villarreal, Sr.	Beverly Marks	Stan Kuper
Connie Garcia	David Fettner	Molly Cordeau
Mr Khera	Ed Childers	Matt Haidenyak
Sheila Childers	Rudy Mayer	Julio Fernandez
James Kuehn	Steve & Paddy Warman	Kevin Johnson

(Your Name Here Next Month)

Side 3—Referral Corner

I'm drowning in debt!!

Just a quick note to let you know how we helped someone and can do the same for you or someone you refer to us!! This is a continuing series of successes from Wes Cordeau.

We just refinanced a family that seven years ago had horrible credit, but worked hard to re-establish and maintain good credit. That was good, however, their credit was so good, the credit card companies gave them **mega amounts** of credit at 22-26%. You know what happened, they ran their credit sky hi and were having trouble paying it. They were maintaining the minimum balances for now. **They asked if we could help.**

We restructured the loan on their home so that they could retire almost all of the $30,786. in credit card debt. Because they had maintained good credit, we lowered their home interest and of course the credit card debt, AND lowered their outlay by $821 monthly.

WOW, would you like to pay off your credit cards and save $821 monthly like this family?

We are "The Dreammakers"!!

PS: If you know of someone like this we can help, please call me with their phone number. **Wes Cordeau 281-445-1901**

Side 4—Evidence Of Success

XXXXXXXXXXXXXXXXXXXXXXXXXXXXXXXXXXXXXXXXXXXXXXXXXXXXXXXXXXXXXXXXXXXXXX
There you go, two complete newsletters. As can be seen, they are nothing elaborate, but very effective. I'm sure there are many people who could do this strategy better than I have, however the results have been nothing short of phenomenal.

Over a three year period, just this newsletter as one pillar of my business produced $1,200,000 in personal revenue for a $5,000 annual investment for printing, postage and outsourcing. An 80-1 return is better than any investment I know of! This newsletter has been a tremendous godsend to us!

Onward we go, learning more how to be a highly paid professional mortgage loan officer!

**If you have an interest in joining this dynamic team, call
281-445-1901, X204 for the "President's Hotline"
or
Email: Wes@TexasSupremeMortgage.com**

Wholesale Lenders Are Your Friends!

Mortgage Broker or Mortgage Banker??   Which is best?

I have been a Mortgage Broker for almost 12 years, and was with a banker for over 4 years. Both environments have their benefits and detriments. I personally like being a broker best because of the flexibility and ability to deliver a loan to the consumer at an OVERALL lower rate and fees than a banker can usually deliver the same loan. Although, some banks will make exceptions that even their wholesale lending area can't match, it is a rarity!

I'll give one example: A "big bank" we are associated with has a retail and wholesale presence. One of my past clients was refinancing his home, and also happened to have a substantial amount of cash on deposit with the bank. His current mortgage was already at this "big bank" from our original purchase money loan two years before.

I had him already qualified. He was in the bank and mentioned what a great deal we were getting him on his refinance—1/2% lower rate than the bank had posted. The bank officer ended up matching the rate, AND to persuade him to close with the bank directly, waived the title fees of $3,000. We were not allowed to waive those fees, so we ended up losing the loan to the bank. The bank made a business decision to keep the loan, and from their standpoint, this was the correct decision, with little risk of the title having problems from two years prior. This is just one of only a very few instances where the "big bank" could or would complete a transaction better than we could as a broker.

As a broker, our cost of loan production is much lower than the banks due to our limited overhead. Many consumers and real estate agents mistakenly think the brokers costs are higher than the bankers because of the "double fees". This is simply NOT the case when comparing the overall cost of the loan. Most mortgage brokers run a "lean and nice" shop; very seldom do we need to run a "mean" shop! We are generally producing managers and have a hardworking staff ready to serve the customers.

Below is a summary of a recent article concerning this important fact!

Please see very important message below and attachment. The Mortgage Industry is really under attack from all fronts. For this reason, it's very important now to become affiliated with your Association of Mortgage Brokers, the Texas Association of Mortgage Brokers and the National Association of Mortgage Brokers. Together we can overcome all these attacks. If we don't, our business will become a lot more restrictive. e-mail me and I'll send an application form.

NEW STUDY: CONSUMERS PAY LOWER ANNUAL PERCENTAGE RATES WITH MORTGAGE BROKERS, NOT MORTGAGE LENDERS

- *Dr. Gregory Elliehausen of the Georgetown University Credit Research Center presented his findings to a Federal Reserve Board Conference on Thursday, April 7ᵗʰ*
- *Co-authors included Amany El Anshasy of George Washington University and Yoshiaki Shimazaki of Oklahoma State University*

McLean, VA – The National Association of Mortgage Brokers (NAMB) today announced its support of the findings of Dr. Gregory Elliehausen of the Georgetown University Credit Research Center. The report stated that brokers' customers have a lower APR, on average, than bank customers. Dr. Elliehausen presented his findings today to a Federal Reserve Board Conference.

"We commend Dr. Elliehausen's detailed research on this very important topic," said NAMB President Bob Armbruster. "We have always believed that the customer who works with mortgage brokers, especially NAMB-affiliated mortgage brokers, receives some of the most favorable terms possible for mortgages. The findings of this report simply prove what NAMB has known for years."

The conclusions of the report are:

* Estimates indicate that borrowers obtaining subprime mortgages through brokers paid **lower annual percentage rates** than borrowers obtaining subprime mortgages from creditors.

* The results support the hypothesis that through competition, brokers tend to pass their origination cost advantages to the consumer.

* The results challenge the view that loans from brokers are more expensive because of broker steering.

* Although the report's findings will not apply to every individual case, there is an overall price benefit to using brokers.

* The benefits of brokers also appear to hold for vulnerable market segments.

"For consumers, working with a mortgage broker who is affiliated with NAMB is a key tool to help protect oneself against fraud or abusive financial practices," adds Armbruster. "The more consumers know what resources to use, the better informed they will be in getting the best mortgage possible."

The National Association of Mortgage Brokers (NAMB) is the voice of the mortgage broker industry with more than 24,000 members in all 50 states and the District of Columbia. NAMB provides education, certification and government affairs representation for the mortgage broker industry, which originates the majority of residential loans in the United States.

We also have a myriad of wholesale lenders to choose from, which again drives down our total cost to the consumer. The wholesale lenders work as hard for our business as we do for the real estate agents business. We are the lifeline to wholesale account managers and their staffs meeting their production goals. If you run a "clean" broker shop as I do, the wholesale lenders love our business and will work with us to get the loans closed timely and at a fair cost to us and the consumers.

We Love Our Wholesale Lenders and Account Reps!

Many times mortgage brokers think they need to take an adversarial position with their wholesale lenders. An US v THEM mentality! Nothing could be further from the truth. We love our wholesale lenders and account reps. A knowledgeable account rep is a valuable resource that can make your life easy and profitable.

I have one sub-prime rep, Mike Shaffer, which I worked with almost exclusively for seven years. He looked at every sub-prime loan first. If his company could close the loan they did. In seven years, there was only ONE loan that he said they could close that ended up not being able to close at his company. I closed about 95% of my sub-prime loans with his company during that period because I could trust the outcome based on the reps knowledge and direction. This type of rep is a valuable tool to me. This is a rep that can be counted on to know his programs inside and out, and to know how the underwriter thinks and looks at each particular situation. If he didn't know, he would call the underwriter to get guidance on a particular issue. If we ran into a problem on a loan at underwriting, he would work it out with the underwriter based on their prior conversation and understanding.

In these 11+ years of working with wholesale lenders, we have treated the companies and their account reps like kings and queens! We have some rules that are strictly adhered to so that our wholesale lenders can trust us. On "A" or FNMA/Conventional loans we only send a complete package to one lender at a time. This may seem standard, but believe me many brokers send their loan packages to multiple lenders and maybe will lock with one lender, and float with another to see which way the market is moving. The only reason the broker does this is to increase **THEIR** broker yield—not to help the consumer!

We have a total restriction on this type of behavior in the FNMA market. We want our wholesale lenders to trust us, so that if they have a package, and can approve the loan, it will close with them. In the short run, it may cost us a little on each loan, but in the long run our integrity is worth much more than a few dollars on each loan. Plus, we can close the loan more quickly, and get better referrals from the clients! In all these years, I have never moved a FNMA loan for better pricing.

There have been some instances that the borrowers have called requesting a lower rate after they have locked with us, and we have locked with the wholesale lender, but only once have I actually lost a loan to this type of request! It's a pretty easy defense when a borrower calls and wants a lower rate because "he read in the paper that the rates were a 1/4% lower now". The conversation usually goes like this:

Client: Hi Wes, I was just reading in the paper that the rates were a little lower than when I made application.
Me: Really, I haven't really noticed, you mean since you locked your rate at time of application?
Client: Yeah, Wes, it looks like maybe a ¼% lower.

Me: No kidding!

Client: *Yeah, no kidding* (they always stammer and stutter right now—clearing their voice), *do you think we could lower my rate?*

Me: So let me ask you, you just want me to be FAIR—right??

Client: Yeah, fair—that's what I'm asking you for, to be fair? (This is sooo easy)

Me: So before I answer, do you remember me explaining "locking" at application?

Client: Sure, means the rate is set.

Me: So, if the rates had gone up 2%, it would be "fair" to the lender to go ahead and raise the rate you had locked at by the 2%, because we just want to be fair—Right?

Client: No,No, we have a lock—that wouldn't be fair!

Me: So, you see why it wouldn't be fair to the lender to lower your rate now, after you had already locked.

In 16 years, I've only had one loan lost after employing this dialog with borrowers. The key is you must adequately explain "locking" upfront to the borrowers, and be prepared to stand your ground. For full disclosure, I have had maybe 3-4 loans that we went back to the lender and split the rate difference IF the rate had dropped dramatically, maybe ¾% for instance. We must protect the wholesale lenders once a loan is locked and delivered!

We Treat Our Account Reps and Wholesale Lenders Like Kings and Queens!
Over the years, there have been many instances of catering to the reps and lenders so that they will remember, like and respect us as a mortgage broker. This is in addition to delivering clean, well documented files for submission, and following up quickly with closing conditions. Those items are expected!

We have gone above and beyond the standard in several instances. We have for instance:
- Personally, along with a processor delivered and served pizza to the lenders staff to thank them for taking care of our business.
- Sponsored wine and cheese parties-in fact one year, two reps met each other at our party, and ended up happily married.
- Sponsored bus trips to a local gambling casino for the reps, staff and their spouses and/ or "significant others". Food and Spirits were provided, but not gambling losses.
- Personally gave a long stemmed red rose to each lady in the office at our favorite wholesale lenders.
- Written several notes to the "big boss", thanking them for hiring excellent staff members or a particular person that helped us on a particular file. Once, I saw a copy of my note with a note from the Regional Manager in each cubical at the wholesale lenders office. I always try to write this note to the "big boss" two levels up from the person that helped us. Good news rolls downhill easily.
- Inserted chocolate candy in the submission file for the underwriter when we knew she was a "chocoholic" like me!

None of these items are costly, but the paybacks are tremendous. We want the wholesale staff to know who we are when we call, so that our file can be approved and closed with the minimum of problems. These marketing tactics will not make a bad file into a good one, but it gives us just a little edge over the other brokers submitting files to the same lenders. It might mean the difference between the underwriter calling our LO back 1st or 10th after she has been out of the office or in "quiet time" reviewing other files.

LO Training: Working With Wholesale Lenders!

The following information is taught to each LO upon joining our company! This is very important in understanding how to work effectively with the wholesale lenders.

How To Work With Your Wholesaler Lender!!

The purpose of this section is to:

1) **Identify Our Wholesale Lenders**
   Approximately 60 lenders fairly evenly split between "A" and Sub-prime. Get to know **2 each from each category** very well. Get their rate sheets emailed to you on a daily basis. Learn the basics of the lenders programs.

2) **Working With Reps**
   The rep is an extension of the underwriter; however, they can "massage" the file a little more than most underwriters will. The rep should be able to tell you if the file has a chance of being approved under their system. When explaining a file to the rep, **explain all details, good, bad and ugly**. It's better to have a quick NO, than a slow NO!!

3) **Working With Underwriters**
   Most lenders will allow you to talk directly to the underwriter. These people are **not GODS**; you are just as important to them as they are to you. However, have your questions and loan scenario in order before you pick up the phone to call.
   What I find helpful for underwriters and Reps, if you are leaving a message is to give as much detail as possible, AND leave the name of the file too. Nothing is worse that the underwriter calling back, and you don't remember the file and she doesn't know the name. As with the Rep, give the whole story!!

4) **Locking**
   Most **"A"** lenders will allow you to lock online--learn how--it is you or your processor's responsibility to get this loan locked properly. Rates change daily.
   Most **Sub-prime** lenders will have you wait until the file is approved before locking. Check to be sure. Rates change at random, but usually not daily.

5) **Stacking Order**
   Each lender will have a stacking order so that every file that submitted is in a consistent order for their company. You want to adhere to this so that when a file arrives at the lender-they are happy to see it, and know it is in the proper order.
   It is sometimes helpful to have a picture of the family in the file when submitting.
   Sometimes, it's helpful to have a little candy in there too!!!

6) **Submission**
   Make all submission documents readable, "head-up", and in proper order. If you have **extra items** that are not on the stacking order form, include either at the rear or front, or in the section that would be most appropriate. Also, very important, include a cover

Websites That Work!

This chapter was compiled from many sources, however much of it was compiled by Catherine Coy, and posted on The Mortgage Grapevine. Other sources were also used. These URLs were accurate at time of printing; however they are subject to change without notice.

The Mortgage Grapevine is a collection of thousands of mortgage loan officer's ideas, questions and other information. Some ideas are very useful, and some are basic gossip. This is an excellent resource, but don't be offended by some of the writings in the chat room!
http://www.mortgagegrapevine.com

Everything You Ever Wanted to Know About Credit Rehabilitation for Consumers and Their Loan Originators:
http://consumers.creditnet.com/straighttalk/board/forumdisplay.php?s=&forumid=3

**Everything you want to know about the 1003
(and a bunch of other stuff):**
http://www.financeadvocate.com/Loan%20Processing/1003/guide1003.htm

Agency (Fannie Mae, Freddie Mac and FHA) underwriting guidelines
http://www.adfinet.com

HUD Handbooks, Forms and Publications:
http://www.hud.gov/offices/adm/handbks_forms/handbooks2.cfm#hnmlr

Read What Consumers Read:

Mortgage-X
http://mortgage-x.com

The Mortgage Professor
http://www.mtgprofessor.com

Mortgage 101
http://www.mortgage101.com

Mortgage Terminology
http://www.mortgage101.com/partner-scripts/1206.asp?p=mtg101

Mortgage Industry Training:

National Association of Mortgage Brokers Education
http://www.namb.org

Mortgage Scholars
http://www.mortgagescholars.com

Mortgage Bankers Association
http://www.campusmba.com

National Association of Professional Mortgage Women
http://www.napmw.org

School of Mortgage Lending
http://www.schoolofmortgagelending.com

Desktop Originator Mortgage Broker Training
http://www.efanniemae.com.

America's Money Center
http://www.americasmoneycenter.com/University.html

American School of Mortgage Banking
http://www.asmb.com

Internet Originator
http://www.internetoriginator.com/io0583.htm

Mortgage Bankers Association of America Residential Finance Updates
http://www.mbaa.org/resident

FHA Training
http://www.epassbusinesscenter.com/learning/industry.asp

Ellie Mae University
http://www.elliemae.com

WebWorxStudio
http://www.webworxstudio.com/etips/new/education.html

Industry Publications Online:

For daily mortgage news
http://www.nationalmortgagenews.com

Origination News
http://www.originationnews.com

Sam Garcia's Mortgage Daily
http://www.mortgagedaily.com

Inman News
http://www.inman.com

Realty Times
http://www.realtytimes.com

Monthly Mortgage Industry Publications

Mortgage Originator Magazine
http://www.mortgageoriginator.com/FSG/MortgageOriginator/default.htm

Broker Magazine
http://www.nationalmortgagenews.com/subscriptions/strategy_broker.htm

For statistics, index trends and other statistics to help your borrower understand interest rate trends

LION, Inc.
http://www.lioninc.com ($50/month)

Barry Habib's Mortgage Market Guide
http://www.mortgagemarketguide.com ($650/year—a Grapevine favorite! Extra benefit: Kiplinger Letters/Guides for all paid MMG subscribers, available online and free access to Mortgage Scholars)

Funding Reference Sources

Broker Magazine's "Weird Loans"
http://www.weirdloans.com

Scotsman Guide
http://www.ezdesk.com/loanpro/scotsmanguide_sub.htm

Loan Origination Software Training

Byte
http://www.byte-cbc.com

Calyx Point
http://www.calyxsoftware.com/training/index.asp

Contour (Loan Handler)
http://www.epassbusinesscenter.com/learning/los_con.asp

Genesis
http://www.genesis2000.com

Loan Originator Success Coaching

Joe Stumpf By Referral Only
http://www.byreferralonly.com

The Core Training, Inc.
www.thecore.tv

Top Producer Strategies – by Loan Officers for Loan Officers
http://www.topproducerstrategies.com

Todd Duncan
http://www.theduncangroup.com

Brian Sacks
http://www.loanofficersuccess.com

Real Estate University
http://www.realestate.university.com

Brian Buffini Providence Seminars
http://www.providenceseminars.com

Mortgage Professional Tools

Tim Braheen's Loan Tool Box

http://www.loantoolbox.com

Loan Magic (voted the best by GrapeViners)
http://www.docmagic.com/products/loanmagic.jsp

Loan Vibe
http://www.loanvibe.com/

EZ Desk
http://www.ezdesk.com

The Mortgage Coach
http://www.wowtools.com

WebWorxStudio
http://www.webworxstudio.com

Internet Marketing

The National Mortgage News Buyer's Guide
http://www.nationalmortgagenews.com/buyersguide/

Mortgage Promote
http://www.mortgagepromote.com

Jeff Lazerson's "How to Make a Fortune in Loans Without Leaving Your Desk"
http://www.lazerson.com/LOAN/book.htm

Shel Horowitz' "Frugal Marketing"
http://www.frugalmarketing.com

Mortgage Leads: If you "Google" Purchase Mortgage Leads, there will be thousands of sources to pop up for your perusal! Who knows if any of them are any good! These lead companies are not being endorsed here or anywhere else in this book. This is just an example of the many sources that are available!

How to Get the Most Out of Internet Leads
http://www.mortgagemag.com/tcse/leadvend.htm

leadz4U@hotmail.com
http://listsareus.com/1-telemarketing-lists-mortgage.htm
http://www.mleads.com
http://www.globalmarketingleads.com

http://www.dataquick.com
http://www.mortgagelinks.org
http://www.mymortgagenavigator.com/mortgage_advertising.htm

Books about mortgages and the mortgage business (all available at amazon.com)

"How to Save Thousands on Your Home Mortgage" by Randy Johnson

"Home Buying for Dummies" by Eric Tyson

"Real Estate Loan Brokerage: How to Become a Successful Mortgage Broker" by Richard B. Partain

"Steiner's Complete How-To-Talk Mortgage Talk"
by Shari and Clyde Steiner

Laws you should know about: To protect yourself and your customers' information

http://www.ftc.gov/bcp/conline/pubs/buspubs/safeguards.htm
The Right to Financial Privacy Act 12 USC 3401 et seq.

The Gramm-Leach-Biley Act 15 USC 6801 et seq.
http://www.fcc.gov/

World's Largest Referral Organization
http://www.bni.com

Down Payment Assistance Programs (DAPs)
None of these are being endorsed, and there are hundreds of other DAP's to select.
The fees will usually range from $295 to ¾% of the loan amount!

1. The Ameridream Charity
http://www.ameridreamcharity.org
2. The Nehemiah Program
http://www.getdownpayment.com
3. The Buyer's Fund Neighborhood Gold
http://www.thebuyersfund.com
4. The Genesis Program
http://www.thegenesisprogram.org

5. Realty America
http://www.realtyamerica.org
6. Home Gift USA http://www.homegiftusa.org
7. Housing Assistance Corporation Local in Florida only
http://www.haconcapecod.org/
8. Partners In Charity
http://www.partnersincharity.org
9. Home Quest
http://www.homequestdownpayment.org
10. Cornerstone Grant
http://www.cornerstonegrant.org
11. Hart
http://www.hartprogram.com
12. Gift America Program
http://www.downpaymentprograms.com
13. American Family Funds
http://www.americanfamilyfunds.com
14. A New Horizon
http://www.anewhorizon.com
15. Apollo Housing
http://www.apollohousingllc.com
16. Alliance Housing Assistance Program
http://www.allianceassistance.org
19. Futures
http://www.fhap.org
18. Home Ownership Providers
http://www.hop-downpayments.org
19. C-Cap Inc.
http://www.c-cap.com
20. Equity Grants
http://www.equitygrants.com

Onward we go, learning more how to be a highly paid professional mortgage loan officer!

**If you have an interest in joining this dynamic team, call
281-445-1901, X204 for the "President's Hotline"
or
Email: Wes@TexasSupremeMortgage.com**

Funny Stories

Every loan officer during the course of their interaction with clients, Real Estate Agents, Underwriters and the general public has some funny stories. These are a few of mine and some borrowed from other friends in the business.

Usually, out of these stories comes a lesson in communication or human nature!

The Literal Lady

Prior to a client coming for a loan application, I try to discuss the information required and any funds that are needed for application. I told this lady that she would need $77.00 for the credit report now and $350.00 for the appraisal when she found her home to purchase. She showed up with most of her documentation, and we had a lovely application and interview. When it came time for the funds that were needed, she brought out a thick envelope.

I asked her what was in there. She says' "it's the $77.00 you needed". She had brought 77, one dollar bills for the application! They were gladly accepted!

That's why we call her, "The Literal Lady!"

Mr. C.D. Man

As above, I had explained the documentation required to this young man prior to the application. He arrived with an armload of information. Upon completing the application, I try to ask the client if there was anything else they have that I failed to ask for during the application. I asked this young man, and he said, "No you have it all except for my CDs-you failed to ask about those." I was actually relieved that he had more cash available, because at application he was a little short of funds.

He opened up this square black box and proceeded to show me his collection of 24 very nice Compact Disc's of various musical artists! When I had told him to bring his bank statements, IRAs, any 401K's and CDs, he interpreted the bank CDs as musical Compact Discs. We both got a good laugh from this, and it taught me a lesson on explaining items required in more details, rather than in our language.

Mr. C.D Man is now a happy homeowner with a major sound system I'm quite sure!

The "Aura Man"

A young man came in with his girlfriend for a loan application one morning. All went pretty much as expected. This was an odd couple, he reminded me of a 1960's hippy, and she could have been a current reigning beauty queen. As discussed in an earlier chapter, I try to take three pictures of each applicant at application, and then again at closing.

In this case, I took out my trusty 35MM camera as always, turned it on, it takes 3 seconds to warm up. This young man protests as many do, "Oh don't take my picture", then snap, snap, snap, I take their picture while explaining what it's for! Usually they are all smiles and everyone is happy! It's just a friendly and helpful touch to the application.

Not This Time!

He came unglued! He's up out of his chair after the first picture, and basically shouts, "I told you **NOT** to take my picture, and now you've done it over my objection". I stopped before the second "snap". What, "I thought you were kidding", I said sort of sheepishly and apologetically. No, he stammers, "Do you know what pictures do to us? Each picture taken destroys part of our Aura! Don't take my picture again". OK!!

I didn't!

The "Aura Man" still owns his condo and is still speaking and referring clients to me, but don't take his picture!

A Family And A Steak

I met this family from India at one of my best Realtor's offices. The loan application and detail work was arduous. We made it thru the application, and I had one of their four children help me make copies. Whew, finally we were finished with the application. It had been over two hours since we began the application process.

So, in my big old jovial Texas attitude, I announce to the family, "You've really worked hard today Mr. Patel, why don't you take your family out for a big steak dinner and really enjoy yourself, while we begin the processing of your loan"! They just half smiled at the Realtor and myself, and left without saying too much.

About 5 minutes later my Realtor friend was laughing uncontrollably. What, what, I ask? Do you realize that in India, Cows are sacred animals! You just invited this lovely family to eat their sacred cow for lunch in celebration of trying to get a new home!

Whoops!

The "Loan App" Man

One day my wife, Molly and I were discussing how long a "generation" is in relation to families. She said, I think a generation is about 70 years.
Nope, I stated, a generation is 20 or so years. Our two boys, Brian and Brad were listening in on the conversation. They were about 12 and 10 years old. Almost in unison, they piped up; I think Mom is right, because she's a teacher. Yeah, and you're just a "loan app man".

They get that from me taking so many "loan apps"!

BTW: Of course we all know that a generation is in fact approximately 20 years, just like the "loan app" man said!

"The Inexperience of Experience"

I was at a closing one fine June morning, and stepped outside the closing room for a few minutes. I was approached by a Realtor that I recognized, but didn't know. She knew that I was a loan officer, but didn't know me personally. She was mad as a hornet. She says, "I need to ask you a question right now". Ok, what can I do for you today, I answered.

How many months does your mortgage company "charge" for taxes at closing? Well, its three months, but then you have to figure in the Aggregate Adjustment, I started to tell her---That's what I thought, she says. Well this mortgage company is charging nine months taxes here at closing. She's yelling now, I've been in this business 20 years, and have never had such a rip-off. I'm never going to use them again for ripping off my poor little clients. Not wanting to correct her then, I just chimed in, "those bastards"; I can't believe they are doing that! I don't blame you, use us instead!

Here's the point. She evidently had 20 years experience, but it may have been the same month, over and over again! On the closing statement for a property closing in June (In Texas) with an escrow account, you in fact record nine months taxes as being "charged" to the buyer on page 2. However, on page 1, is a credit from the seller for the six months of the year the seller owned the property. So, the net effect is three months taxes being put into escrow, on behalf of the buyer, by the buyer, and six months by the seller, on behalf of the buyer.

I did not pursue her business after that encounter!

"You Work For Whom"?

This lady called me one day and asked if I could get her a mortgage if her credit was not too perfect, as she described it. We can certainly take a look and determine if you can purchase a home I replied. I asked her who she was working for, and she replied, "The Welfare Department". Oh, OK, and how long have you worked there? She replied, 22 years. Wow, that's a long time, and she agreed. I then asked her how much she earned, to which she replied $600. OK, I said, that's $600, weekly, or about $2,500 monthly. I think you could qualify on this home purchase.

She says, no, I earn $600 monthly. Are you working part-time, I ask, she says no, it's full-time and paid monthly. Thinking, I'll get back to this question, I went on to get information about her residence, bank accounts and other information. Finally, I asked about employment and wages again. She assured me that it was $600 monthly, not weekly.

Still thinking that I was misinterpreting something, I pointed out that minimum wage is more than $600 monthly. She replies, I don't know why they don't pay me more.
Still perplexed, I asked her one more time in another way, Maam, I asked, "Are you working for the welfare department, or are you on welfare assistance?" She responds, "It's all the same to me, they give me a check every month, but they deliver it to my apartment".

Finally, I could see the light, she was on government assistance. This would not preclude her from buying a home, however with $600 monthly income; it would severely limit her ability to purchase a home.

"It Was A Banging Experience"

One of my personal favorite clients called me to get a new loan for himself. I inquired as to how he and his wife were doing. They had been one of the sweetest couples I had ever worked with in the lending business, and easiest too because of great credit and their good jobs.

He informed me that they weren't together anymore. Too bad, I thought.

He also told me that the home they had previously financed together was in arrears now, and let's take a look at his overall credit to determine whether we could lend just to him.

Upon reviewing his credit, it was perfect except for about 4 months prior, every payment was late for two months, and had recently been made current. I asked him what had happened during this period?

He informed me that he was in the hospital for a month during that period and couldn't work for two more months! I asked him for more details, so we could help write the letter on credit to the underwriter. He told me the WHOLE story!

The husband had found out prior to filing for divorce that his wife was having an affair with the neighbor next to the home they had jointly purchased a few years before. He went over to confront the next door neighbor. My client got in an altercation with the neighbor. The neighbor beat the daylights out of him, and put him in the hospital for a month. The neighbor went to jail, and my client filed for divorce!

So in writing the letter of credit to the underwriter, I said that the late payments were due to the hospital stay and incapacity to work in those three months. Basically I wrote to the underwriter, "that the neighbor was banging my client's wife, and him, and please take this into account when reviewing his otherwise perfect credit history!"

The underwriter called a day or so later and told me that was the most creative explanation she had ever read and they made an exception on the file to get it approved!

He is now a happy single homeowner!

"It was a long long time ago"

In January, 1995, this lady called about purchasing a home, but she mentioned that she and her husband had a Chapter 7 Bankruptcy, but it was a long, long time ago! I responded, "Well, when was it discharged, because that is the date we use to determine the starting point and at that time we needed to wait approximately 2 years to get a new mortgage." I asked her if she had the paperwork readily available.

She begins asking her husband to help her remember when the Bankruptcy was discharged. He says, "Man that was a long time ago"! I still needed to know exactly when, but I'm feeling pretty comfortable that it was more than two years in the past.

Finally, I hear rustling papers, and she says, "OK, we have the discharge papers right here. Oh yes, it was a long, long time ago!" I can see a new loan application ready to come in for sure now! Finally, she says, "Yup, it was discharged in July, 1994", that was so long ago, I can't hardly remember it"!

So it was six months ago, I asked her? Yeah, a long, long time ago, she states!

"We're Getting A D-I-V-O-R-C-E"

Late one Friday afternoon, I had a closing across town. Unfortunately, I was not able to go to this closing. However, I had spoken to the Realtors and the buyers, all seemed to be in order, then I left for the weekend. Early Monday morning, I called the title company closer, and ask how was closing, everything went Ok, I'm sure?

Oh, you haven't heard, she says! (That's a bad sign on a early Monday morning) I've never had this situation before, the closer says, and sort of half laughing! The buyers came in and seemed to be OK with all the paperwork. Before we started signing, the wife started crying. So I tried to console her, and ask her if she needed anything to drink. No, the buyer stammers. Well, are you just nervous about all the paperwork? No, she says. Well, maybe if you are depleting your savings and buying this first home, it's somewhat distressing? No, the buyer's wife says. Finally, the closer mentions that some buyers get real nervous over making a 30 year commitment, and maybe that is upsetting this young woman? Again, No the buyer says!

By this time, "I was somewhat perplexed myself" the closer says, to me. So finally, she says, I asked the buyer, what can I do to help you? The wife reaches into her purse, and pulls out a bundle of paperwork. She is now in almost uncontrollable tears, but manages to blurt out, "Honey, I love the house, but I want a Divorce instead". She then proceeds to ask the closer to please notarize the delivery of the Divorce papers to her soon-to-be-ex husband!

The closer was stunned, but did notarize the documents that the husband had been served the papers, and had several witnesses!

Obviously, this did not result in a happy homeowner!

"The Car Was For Running Around"

In explaining past due credit issues, we try to shed as favorable a light on the derogatory credit as possible, yet give a truthful explanation. I was working with a young man, a navy veteran of 4 years. His vessel had been stationed in Pensacola Florida, if I remember correctly. He had been out of the Navy for about 18 months, when we were introduced.

Upon reviewing his credit report, he had flawless credit, except for an auto repossession about 30 months prior. There was an outstanding balance of several thousands of dollars. I quizzed him on this, because it seemed like an anomaly in his otherwise perfect credit. Thinking it was probably a mistake or a relative with a similar name, this would be easy to explain and get corrected.

Not quite!

He proceeded to tell me that he would never pay for this auto, and he had a legitimate reason for letting the car go to repossession. He had bought this car for his wife while he was on sea maneuvers for 12 months so she could go running around town. Well, she ended up "running around" with his best friend from Pensacola. Upon returning and finding out the situation, he filed for divorce and quit paying notes on the car.

So, ultimately, I suggested, that he had bought the car for his wife to go running around in, and she did just that! Fortunately, we were able to explain this situation and he ended up being a happy homeowner!

A Home With A Family!
This story was contributed by Max Townsend. Thanks for your input Max!

Last year, I helped a guy purchase a home with acreage. As he was in the negotiation stage with the seller, he called me to get pre-qualified, no Realtors or advisors involved. I was able to qualify him and sent him a letter stating such. After getting the agreement signed, this guy was so anxious to move into his new house and settle into his new role, he went ahead and ordered 3 cows, 2 goats, 1 horse and a dozen chickens. .. . To be delivered in a week! I don't know how you "order" these things but he called me up and asked how quickly we could close the loan as he had an important delivery coming. He had no idea of the time it would take to process the loan, get title and appraisal, etc – in rural NY. Needless to say he was scrambling to find a place for the animals and I was getting a daily status inquiry call. Although he ended up getting the seller to lease him part of his future property for about a week so the big animals had a place to stay, they didn't have chicken coops and he ended up having to keep the chickens in his house until he could move. . . . .

I think he now understands the difference between pre-qualifying and funding!

Onward we go, learning more how to be a highly paid professional mortgage loan officer!

**If you have an interest in joining this dynamic team, call
281-445-1901, X204 for the "President's Hotline"
or
Email:** Wes@TexasSupremeMortgage.com

"Cordeauisms"

This is a compilation of statements and affirmations that have been useful to me over my life. I started working and compiling this list in 1975! Very little here is new, but all were and are meaningful to me. I have attributed these statements to people I have learned them from, if known. Some of my favorite people to use information from are Tony Robbins, Jim Rohn, Joe Stumpf, Les Brown, Zig Ziglar, and many others.

These statements are in no particular order, and the list is continually growing and evolving.

Pick out the top 10 affirmations that are meaningful to you. Combine these affirmations with your current goals. Laminate several copies and keep a copy in your car, in your bathroom, in your daily planner and in your right hand desk drawer, unless you are left handed. Keep these where you WILL see and read these statements and goals daily!

If you **always** worry about money,
You'll **always** worry about money!
If you **always** worry about your client,
You will **NEVER** worry about money!
John Stapleton

People want your Hope, More than your Success!

The 5 "S's" of Life!

Scarcity:	This stage of "S's" is where you just aren't making it financially Having to borrow money to stay afloat, depleting savings, maxing out credit cards-just not making ends meet.
Stability:	In this stage of "S's", you are just barely making ends meet. You are praying that the car doesn't break down, or the kids don't get sick. You're nose is just above the water line!
Success:	In this stage, you are finally doing OK. You are able to pay all your bills on time, you are able to fully fund your retirement accounts and pay for and take those much needed vacations. Most people are satisfied and "park" at this level.
Service:	In this stage, everything in "Success" is still being accomplished, however in this stage you are also able to freely give away some of your earnings and feel comfortable about the giving.
Significance:	In this final stage, everything in Success and Service is still being accomplished. However in this stage, you set up a formal plan or foundation to continue you're legacy after you are gone from this earth!

The Past does Not equal the Future!

Don't let your **"Highs"** get too high, or the **"Lows"** too low!

The Louder you Scream, the Less I hear!

People Form Habits!
Habits Form Futures!

Massive Passionate Action will insure Success

Love of Vocation is like being on a Vacation at all times!

I'm not trying to IMPRESS you, I'm trying to impress UPON you these ideas!

Clarity of Purpose is Pure Power!

The road to "Someday" leads to a town of "Nowhere"!

Will, wins over Skill---Every time!

Adversity is the Mother of Invention!

Action Cures Fear!

Late to Bed,
Early to Rise,
Work like Hell,
And Advertise

The "I Will" is much more important than the "I Q"!

Failure only comes by not trying to the best of your ability!

Perception is Stronger than Reality!

Just Do It!

Do It Now!

Motion Will Change Emotion!

Live Life With Passion!

Live Life With An Attitude Of Gratitude!

There is a Way, If I am Truly Committed!

Lack of planning on YOUR part, does not Constitute an Emergency on my part!

What the mind can see, can be accomplished, If you are inspired!

Don't spend your time watching others make it in sports!
Put as much effort into your "sport" of business, as you would supporting the "team"!

Purpose is Stronger than Outcome!!   Reasons come First, then Answers!

Many people die at 21, but don't get buried until age 70! (Les Brown)

Have you parked in life at a comfortable level, Instead of moving forward?

When you are willing to do whatever it takes to succeed, legally,
Then you won't have to! Your mind will free up a way for success.

Dissatisfaction Creates Power!

What Is Your "Why" In Life?

The Harder I Work, The Luckier, I get!

Be judged on whether you WIN or LOSE, but not be accused of NOT TRYING!
Jim Rohn

You attract unto yourself the equivalent of that which you express!

Birds of a feather flock together!

The Riches are in the Niches!

Unless You Change How You Are, You'll Always Have What You've Got, *Jim Rohn*

Goals become Power when you have an Absolute Total Belief and Faith in the Outcome!

Excuses take more Energy than Action!

B	Basic	F	Find
I	Instruction	A	Answers
B	Before	I	In
L	Leaving	T	The
E	Earth	H	Heart

Belief is the Feeling of a Certainty about the outcome!

Cure "Excutitus" with fervent Action!

Our Emotions are not our Identities!

Repetition is the Mother of all Skill!

Expect the Best and it will Happen!

What would you be Willing to Try, If you knew you Would Not Fail?

Confidence Comes Before Competence!

Be thankful for Problems! Problems make you Grow!

Problems are actually Opportunities in Disguise!

FEAR = False Evidence Appearing Real!

FORD = Fix Or Repair Daily!

FORD = First On Race Day!

I expect you to expect First Class Service from me!

You never have a Permanent Win or Loss!

Winning is not a Destination, but a Lifelong Journey!

Winning is a Daily Activity!

Jesus was the best Network Marketer ever. He would present the "PLAN".
If you Accepted the Plan, you received the Goods and Glory.
If you Rejected the Plan, you could go to Hell!

As Further Evidence Of Jesus Being The Best Network Marketer,
We are still promoting His Plan 2000 Years after his death!

We do not Plan to Fail, but Fail to Plan!

Massive Passionate Action will return Massive Passionate Results!

You may be Disappointed if you Fail, But you are Doomed if you Don't Try!
Beverly Sills

What YOU focus on expands, either for Good or for Bad!

Focus on what you want, Not what you don't want!

There is no pillow as soft as a Clear Conscience!

Hire Character and Desire, before Skills!

TRY = Tomorrow is Really Yesterday

Clients remember High Quality and Great Service
Long after the Low Price has Worn Off!

Never negotiate out of Fear, but never Fear to Negotiate!

Progress Always Includes Risk!

It is not how Hard you Fall, but How High you Bounce Back!
Charlie "Tremendous" Jones

You can't be a Winner, If you are a Whiner!

Whiners are not Winners!

Don't waste my time, It can't be replaced!

Steal my money, but not my time!

Don't Spend Major Time with Minor People!

People that are Going Nowhere, Want you to go Nowhere with Them!

You can choose to be a Champ, or a Chump!

To put yourself on the path to succeed, you must take Total Responsibility!

Do you Miss Opportunities because you are Too Focused on Obstacles?

He who dares Nothing, Need not Hope for Anything!

Desire and Hope are of no Benefit without "Doing"!

Goals Must Be: Well Defined
Realistic
Meaningful

Able to Visualize
Exciting
Have An Action Plan
Acted Upon

What you Resist, Will Persist, What you Embrace, You can Control

Straight "A's" = Attitude, Aptitude, Action, Accountability

The Past is History, The Future is a Mystery
The Present is a Gift, We must use it Wisely

Massive Action Equals Massive Income

Your mind will Obey any Instructions you give it!

If it's to Be, It's up to Me!

FAMILY = (F)ather (A)nd (M)other (I) (L)ove (Y)ou.

Being Broke is a Temporary Situation. Being Poor is a Mental State

"G R E A T" =   **G**oal Orientated
                   Results Orientated
                   Excellence
                   Action
                   Time Organization

Annual Checkup From The Neck up:
- Where have I been so far in my life?
- Why am I here right now?
- Where am I headed this year?
- Why am I headed there?
- Has life given me what I'm looking for?
- Am I challenging myself?
- Is my life an adventure, or boring?

No Occupation will be Over Crowded with Highly Qualified People
Who have a Burning Desire to Succeed and Perform!

Professional:
Someone who makes the Job look so Simple that Anyone could do it with Ease!

People are Concerned about the Needs of Others,
But they are Motivated to Action by their Own Needs and Desires

The most famous radios station in America is:
WIFM: What's In It For Me!

Average is the Worst of the Best,
And the Best of the Worst!

Converting Possibilities into Realities will Always Require Risk!

WORK to meet your Needs, but DREAM to Get Ahead!

The Path of Least Resistance, Rarely Leads to Success!

A Person who Believes in you is a Tremendous Source of Power!

Love People, Use Things, NOT Vice Versa!

The more we Respect our Buyer, the More they will Buy!

Your Client Doesn't Care How Much You Know,
Until They Know How Much You Care!

Shoot for the Moon and the Stars, If you miss, you're still high!

You have to take a lot of Swings to hit a lot of Home Runs!

You Alone are Responsible for Your Attitudes,
And You Alone can make them More Positive!

Successful Entrepreneurs have Tremendous Tenacity in Common!

Your Vision of Success is Ever Changing,
It will be Different Ten years from Now,
As it was Ten years in the Past!

The Single Greatest Deterrent to Achieving Success is Looking at the Great Chasm
Between Where You are Now and Where you Want to be, and Doing Nothing!

STP = See The People

You Can Make Money or You Can Make Excuses,
But, You Can't Do Both!

Would You Ever Talk To Your Best Friend,
The Same Way We Sometimes Talk To Ourselves?

The world is composed of three types of people:
1) The Haves
2) The Have Not's
3) The Have Not Paid For What They Have

Fear Can Stir up a Strong Desire to Succeed!

Flight or Fight!

Some people are addicted to suffering! Stay away from them!

Self-Esteem is Based on WHO You Are, Not WHAT You Have!

Failure Follows Those Who Fail to Follow Through!

Positive Power Thinking People Expect To See Difficulties,
But Also Expect To Overcome Them!

Power Thinkers are "Successed Out", not Stressed Out!

Power Thinking Is Acting As If We Are What We Wish We Were Already!

How Sweet it is to Stand on the Edge of Tomorrow!

When Proof is Possible, Faith Becomes Impossible!

Tough Times Never Last, but Tough people Do!
Robert Schuller

It's Impossible to Fail Completely, and it's Impossible to Succeed Perfectly!

If God is For You, Who Could Be Against You!

Whatever You Give Away Will Come Back To You, Multiplied!

Success Without Conflict Is Unrealistic!

If you don't have Dreams beyond your Grasp, You've already begun to Die!

True Character is the ability to carry out Goals, Long after the "Mood" has Passed!

FORD: Talk with all contacts using this formula!

F	Family
O	Occupation
R	Recreation
D	Dreams

The Cost of Education is NOT as Expensive as the Cost of Ignorance!

Worry is the Interest you Pay, on a Loan you May Never Receive!

Fear is a Motivating Factor!

Everyone Experiences Fear!

Ever Notice That the People Who Are The Most Thankful, Appreciative, and Grateful, Have the Most To Be Thankful, Appreciative and Grateful About!

Truth is Only Discovered in Times of Difficulty!

FOCUS
Foresight/Faith
Organization
Courage
Understanding
Seeding/Service

Money is a By-Product of Other Achievements!

Adversity Builds Character!

Winners Don't Give Up, They Get Up!

Self Motivation = Work = Success

We need GOALS to keep us going

G	Gather Information
O	Organize
A	Act
L	Look and Learn
S	Set New Goals

Plan for What is Difficult, When it is Easy!

Everyone's Biggest Fear is the Fear of Failure, unless
Their Biggest Fear Is the Fear Of Success!!

The Biggest Mistake People Make is Dwelling on Past Mistakes!

Action Plan:
1.   Write 10 goals for this year
2.   Choose most important goal
3.   Write 20 reasons to accomplish that goal
4.   Write plan for achieving goal

The More We Give, The More We Receive!

EGO = Edge God Out

Attitudes form Beliefs
Beliefs form Behavior
Behavior forms Habits
Habits form Routines
Routines form Results
Results form Lives

Become part of some one else's Miracle!

Feeling off track?   Help someone else to get on track!

Character is our Toughest Part of who we are!

Excuses Keep Us From Taking Action and Learning!

The Difference between being Awesome, and being Awful, is Service To Clients!

If you talk about it, It's a dream!
If you envision it, It's possible!
If you schedule it, It's a reality!

What you think about, you talk about!
What you talk about, you walk about!
What you walk about, you are!

Almost Any System Will Work, IF You Work The System

Onward we go, learning more how to be a highly paid professional mortgage loan officer!

If you have an interest in joining this dynamic team, call
281-445-1901, X204 for the "President's Hotline"
or
Email: Wes@TexasSupremeMortgage.com

The Final Thoughts!

You have endured my musings for this far. Hopefully you have learned enough to become a better loan officer and person too by reading this book. You can see now, that this business is really not that difficult to learn, if you have the desire to do so.

Good luck in all your endeavors.

Glossary Of Mortgage Terms

Acceleration Clause-
The right of the mortgage (lender) to demand the immediate repayment of the mortgage loan balance upon the default of the mortgagor (borrower), or by using the right vested in the Due-on-Sale Clause

Adjustable Rate Mortgage(ARM)-
Is a mortgage in which the interest rate is adjusted periodically based on a pre-selected index. Also sometimes known as the re-negotiable rate mortgage or the Canadian rollover mortgage

Adjustment Interval-
On an adjustable rate mortgage, the time between changes in the interest rate and/or monthly payment, typically one, three, or five years, depending on the index.

Amortization-
Means loan payment by equal periodic payment calculated to pay off the debt at the end of a fixed period, including accrued interest on the outstanding balance

Annual Percentage Rate A.P.R.-
Is an interest rate reflecting the cost of a mortgage as a yearly rate. This rate is likely to be higher than the stated note rate or advertised rate on the mortgage, because it takes into account points and other credit costs. The APR allows home buyers to compare different types of mortgages based on the annual cost for each loan.

Appraisal
An estimate of the value of property, made by a qualified professional called an "appraiser" assessment. A local tax levied against a property for a specific purpose, such as a sewer or street lights.

Assumption-
The agreement between buyer and seller where the buyer takes over the payments on an existing mortgage from the seller. Assuming a loan can usually save the buyer money since this is an existing mortgage debt, unlike a new mortgage where closing cost and new, probably higher, market-rate interest charges will apply.

Balloon (payment) mortgage-
Usually a short-term fixed-rate loan which involves small payments for a certain period of time and one large payment for the remaining amount of the principal at a time specified in the contract.

Blanket Mortgage-
A mortgage covering at least two pieces of real estate as a security for the same mortgage.

Borrower (Mortgagor)-
One who applied for and receives a loan in the form of a mortgage with the intention of repaying the loan in full.

Broker-
An individual in the business of assisting in arranging funding or negotiating contracts for a client buy who does not loan the money himself. Brokers usually charge a fee or receive a commission for their services.

Buy-down-
The action to pay additional discount points(buy down subsidy) to the lender in exchange for a lower interest rate. The reduced rate may apply for all or a portion of the loan term. This subsidy amount may be paid by the buyer, lender, seller or a combination of parties.

Cash Flow
The amount of cash derived over a certain period of time from an income-producing property. The cash flow should be large enough to pay the expenses of the income producing property (mortgage payment, maintenance, utilities, etc..)

Caps (interest)
Consumer safeguards which limit the amount the interest rate on an adjustable rate mortgage may change per year and/or the life of the loan.

Caps (payment)
Consumer safeguards which limit the amount monthly payments on an adjustable rate mortgage may change.

Certificate of Eligibility
The document given to qualified veterans which entitles them to VA guaranteed loans for homes, business, and mobile homes. Certificates of eligibility may be obtained by sending DD-214 (Separation Paper) to the local VA office with VA form 1880 request for Determination of Eligibility

Certificate of Reasonable Value (CRV)
A certification for an appraisal issued by the Veterans Administration showing the property's current marked value.

Certificate of veteran status
The document given to veterans or reservists who have served 90 days of continuous active duty (including training time) or 6 years in the reserves. It may be obtained by sending DD 214 to the local VA office with form 26-8261a (request for the certificate of veteran status). This document enables veterans to obtain lower down payments on certain FHA insured loans

Closing

The meeting between the buyer, seller and lender or their agents where the property and funds legally change hands. Also called settlement. Closing costs usually include an origination fee, discount points, appraisal fee, title search and insurance, survey, taxes, deed recording fee, credit report charge and other costs assessed at settlement. The costs of closing usually are about 3 percent to 6 percent of the mortgage amount.

Co Borrower (co signer, co mortgagor)

One who signs a mortgage contract with another party or parties and is hereby jointly obligated to repay the loan. Generally a co borrower provides some assistance in meeting the requirements of the loan, and receives a share of interest in the encumbered property.

Commitment

An agreement, often in writing, between a lender and a borrower to loan money at a future date subject to the completion of paperwork or compliance with stated conditions.

Commitment

A promise by a lender to make a loan on specific terms or conditions to a borrower or builder. A promise by an investor to purchase mortgages from a lender with specific terms or conditions.

Construction loan (interim loan)

A loan to provide the funds necessary to pay for the construction of buildings or homes. These are usually designed to provide periodic disbursements to the builder as he progresses. Contract sale or deed: A contract between purchaser and a seller of real estate to convey title after certain conditions have been met. It is a form of installment sale.

Construction loan

A short term interim loan for financing the cost of construction. The lender advances funds to the builder at periodic intervals as the work progresses.

Conventional loan

A mortgage not insured by FHA or guaranteed by the VA.

Credit Report

A report documenting the credit history and current status of a borrower's credit standing

Debt-to-Income Ratio (DTI)

The ratio, expressed as a percentage, which results when a borrower's monthly payment obligation on long-term debts is divided by his or her net effective income (FHA/VA loans) or gross monthly income (conventional loans). See housing expenses-to-income ratio.

Deed of trust
In many states, this document is used in place of a mortgage to secure the payment of a note.

Default
Failure to meet legal obligations in a contract, specifically, failure to make the monthly payments on a mortgage.

Deferred interest
When a mortgage is written with a monthly payment that is less than required to satisfy the note rate, the unpaid interest is deferred by adding it to the loan balance. See negative amortization

Delinquency
Failure to make payments on time. This can lead to foreclosure.

Department of Veterans Affairs (VA)
An independent agency of the federal government which guarantees long-term, low or no-down payment mortgages to eligible veterans.

Discount Point
see Point

Down Payment
Money paid to make up the difference between the purchase price and the mortgage amount. Down payments can range from 3 percent to 20 percent or more of the sales price on conventional loans

Due-On-Interest
A clause inserted in a mortgage that allows the lender to call the loan due and payable at its option upon the transfer of the property also known as paragraph "17 " in FNMA/FHLMC Mortgage.

Due-on-Sale-Clause
A provision in a mortgage or deed of trust that allows the lender on demand immediate payment of the balance of the mortgage if the mortgage holder sells the home.

Earnest Money
Money given by a buyer to a seller as part of the purchase price to bind a transaction or assure payment.

Entitlement
The VA home loan benefit is called entitlement. Entitlement for a VA guaranteed home loan. This is also known as eligibility.

Equal Credit Opportunity Act (ECOA)
Is a federal law that requires lenders and other creditors to make credit equally available without discrimination based on race, color, religion, national origin, age, sex, marital status or receipt of income from public assistance programs.

Equity
The value an owner has in real estate over and above the obligation against the property.

Escrow
Funds that are set aside and held in trust, usually for payment of taxes and insurance on real property. Also earnest deposits held pending loan closing.

Escrow
Refers to a neutral third party who carries out the instruction of both the buyer and seller to handle all the paperwork of settlement or closing. Escrow may also refer to an account held by the lender into which the home buyer pays money for tax or insurance payments.

Fannie Mae
See Federal National Mortgage Association

Farmers Home Administration (FmHA)
Provides financing to farmers and other qualified borrowers who are unable to obtain loans elsewhere.

Federal Home Loan Bank Board (FHLBB)
A regulatory and supervisory agency for federally chartered savings institutions.

Federal Home Loan Mortgage Corporation (FHLMC)
Also called "Freddie Mac". A quasi-governmental agency that purchases conventional mortgage from insured depository institutions and HUD-approved mortgage bankers.

Federal Housing Administration (FHA)
A division of the Department of Housing and Urban Development (HUD). Its main activity is the insuring of residential mortgage loans made by private lenders. FHA also sets standards for underwriting mortgages.

Federal National Mortgage Association (FNMA)
Also known as "Fannie Mae." A private corporation, federally chartered to provide financial products and services that increase the availability and affordability of housing for low-, moderate- and middle-income Americans. The largest corporation in America, Fannie Mae has $287 billion in assets and an additional $544 billion in Mortgage-Backed Securities outstanding. Next to the U.S. Treasury, it is often the second largest borrower in the capital markets. Fannie Mae is traded on the New York Stock Exchange (FNM) and has approximately 190,000 shareholders.

FHA Loan
A loan insured by the Federal Housing Administration open to all qualified home purchasers. While there are limits to the size of FHA loans($155,250), they are generous enough to handle moderately-priced homes almost anywhere in the country.

FHA Mortgage Insurance Premium (MIP)
An amount equal to 2.25 percent of the loan amount paid at closing or financed into the loan amount. In addition, FHA mortgage insurance requires an annual fee of 0.5 percent of the current loan amount, paid in monthly installments. The lower the down payment, the more years the fee must be paid.

FHLMC
The Federal Home Loan Mortgage Corporation provides a secondary market for saving and loans by purchasing their conventional loans. Also known as "Freddie Mac."

Firm Commitment
A promise by FHA to insure a mortgage loan for a specified property and borrower. A promise from a lender to make a mortgage loan.

Fixed Rate Mortgage
The mortgage interest rate will remain the same on these mortgages throughout the term of the mortgage for the original borrower.

FNMA
The Federal National Mortgage Association is a secondary mortgage institution which is the largest single holder of home mortgages in the United States. FNMA buys VA, FHA, and conventional mortgages from primary lenders. Also known as "Fannie Mae."

Foreclosure
A legal process by which the lender or the seller forces a sale of a mortgaged property because the borrower has not met the terms of the mortgage. Also known as a repossession of property.

Freddie Mac
see Federal Home Loan Mortgage Corporation

Ginnie Mae
see Government National Mortgage Association

Government National Mortgage Association (GNMA)
Also known as "Ginnie Mae." Provides sources of funds for residential mortgages, insured or guaranteed by FHA or VA.

Graduated Payment Mortgage (GPM)
A type of flexible-payment mortgage where the payments increase for a specified period of time and then level off. This type of mortgage has negative amortization built into it.

Guaranty
A promise by one party to pay a debt or perform an obligation contracted by another if the original party fails to pay or perform according to a contract.

Hazard Insurance (Homeowners Insurance)
A form of insurance in which the insurance company protects the insured from specified losses, such as a fire, windstorm and the like.

Housing Expenses-to-Income Ratio
The ratio, expressed as a percentage, which results when a borrower's housing expenses are divided by his/her gross monthly income. See debt-to-Income ratio.

Impound
That portion of a borrower's monthly payments held by the lender or servicer to pay for taxes , hazard insurance, mortgage insurance, lease payments, and other items as they become due. Also known as reserves.

Index
A published interest rate against which lenders measure the difference between the current interest rate on an adjustable rate mortgage and that earned by other investments (such as one- , three-, and five-year U.S. Treasury security yields (T-Bills), the monthly average interest rate on loans closed by savings and loan institutions, and the monthly average cost-of-funds incurred by savings and loans), which is then used to adjust the interest rate on an adjustable mortgage up or down.

Investor
A money source for a lender(FNMA, FHLMC, GNMA).

Interim Financing
A construction loan made during completion of a building or a project. A permanent loan usually replaces this loan after completion

Jumbo Loan
A loan which is larger(more than $207,000) than the limits set by the Federal National Mortgage Association and the Federal Home Loan Mortgage Corporation. Because jumbo loans cannot be funded by these two agencies, they usually carry a lighter interest rate.

Lien
A claim upon a piece of property for the payment or satisfaction of a debt or obligation.

LNOV(Lenders Notification Of Reasonable Value)
A certification for an appraisal issued by the Lender in place of a CRV showing the property's current marked value.

Loan-to-Value Ratio (LTV)
The relationship between the amount of the mortgage loan and the appraised value of the property expressed as a percentage.

Margin
The amount a lender adds to the index on an adjustable rate mortgage to establish the adjusted interest rate.

Market Value
The highest price that a buyer would pay and the lowest price a seller would accept on a property. Marked value may be different from the price a property could actually be sold for at a given time.

MIP:Mortgage Insurance Premium
A monthly premium paid by the homeowner in addition to the UP Front MIP that is generally financed. The monthly mortgage insurance is equal to the mortgage amount multiplied by .005 divided by 12. ($100,00 X .005/12=41.67 per month.

Mortgage Insurance
Money paid to insure the mortgage when the down payment is less than 20 percent. See private mortgage insurance, FHA mortgage insurance.

Mortgagee
The Lender

Mortgagor
The borrower or homeowner

Negative Amortization
Occurs when your monthly payments are not large enough to pay all the interest due on the loan. This unpaid interest is added to the unpaid balance of the loan. The danger of negative amortization is that the home buyer ends up owing more than the original amount of the loan.

Net Effective Income
The borrower's gross income minus federal income tax.

Non Assumption Clause
A statement in a mortgage contract forbidding the assumption of the mortgage without the prior approval of the lender.

Note
The signed obligation to pay a debt, as a mortgage note.

Origination Fee
The fee charged by a lender to prepare loan documents, make credit checks, inspect and sometimes appraise a property; usually computed as a percentage of the face value of the loan.

Permanent Loan
A long term mortgage, usually ten years or more. Also called an "end loan."

PITI
Principal, Interest, Taxes and Insurance. Also called monthly housing expense.

Pledged Account Mortgage (PAM)
Money is placed in a pledged savings account and this fund plus earned interest is gradually used to reduce mortgage payments.

Points (loan discount points)
Prepaid interest assessed at closing by the lender. Each point is equal to 1 percent of the loan amount (e.g.. two points on a $100,000 mortgage would cost $2,000). It is also sometimes used to buy down the interest rate, but also is commonly known as Broker Fees for remuneration to the Loan Broker

Power of Attorney
A legal document authorizing one person to act on behalf of another.

Prepaid Expenses
Necessary to create an escrow account or to adjust the seller's existing escrow account. Can include taxes, hazard insurance, private mortgage insurance and special assessments.

Prepayment
A privilege in a mortgage permitting the borrower to make payments in advance of their due date.

Prepayment Penalty
Money charged for an early repayment of debt. Prepayment penalties are allowed in some form (but not necessarily imposed) in 36 states and the District of Columbia.

Primary Mortgage Market
Lenders making mortgage loans directly to borrowers such as a savings and loan association, commercial banks, and mortgage companies. These lenders sometimes sell their mortgages into the secondary mortgage markets such as to FNMA or GNMA, etc.

Principal
The amount of debt, not counting interest, left of a loan.

Private Mortgage Insurance (PMI)
In the event that you do not have a 20 percent down payment, lenders will allow a smaller down payment- as low as 3 percent in some cases. With the smaller down payment loans, however, borrowers are required to carry private mortgage insurance which is generally paid monthly, and obtained by the lender through a Private Mortgage Insurance Company (GE, MGIC, United Guarantee, Amerin, PMI,etc..).

Real Estate Agent or Broker
A licensed real estate agent or broker through the state that is not associated with a local, state or national board of Realtors.

Realtor®
A real estate broker or an associate holding active membership in a local and state real estate board and is affiliated with the National Association of Realtors.

Rescission
The cancellation of a contract. With respect to mortgage refinancing, the law that gives the homeowner three days to cancel a contract in some cases once it is signed if the transaction uses equity in the home as security

Recording Fees
Money paid to the lender for recording a home sale with the local authorities, thereby making it part of the public records.

Refinance
Obtaining a new mortgage loan on a property already owned. Often to replace existing loans on the property.

Negotiable Rate Mortgage (RBM)
A loan in which the interest rate is adjusted periodically. See adjustable rate mortgage.

RESPA
Short for the Real Estate Settlement Procedures Act. RESPA is a federal law that allows consumers to review information on known or estimated settlement cost once after application and once prior to or at a settlement . The law requires lenders to furnish the information after application only.

Reverse Annuity Mortgage (RAM)
A form of mortgage in which the lender makes periodic payments to the borrower using the borrower's equity in the home as Satisfaction of Mortgage: The document issued by the mortgagee when the mortgage loan is paid in full is called a "release of mortgage."

Second Mortgage
A mortgage made subsequent to another mortgage and subordinate to the first one.

Secondary Mortgage Market
The place where primary mortgage lenders sell the mortgages they make to obtain more funds to originate more new loans. It provides liquidity for the lenders security.

Servicing
All the steps and operations a lender performs to keep a loan in good standing, such as a collection of payments, payment of taxes, insurance, property inspections and the like.
Settlement/Settlement Costs
See Closing/Closing Costs

Shared Appreciation Mortgage (SAM)
A mortgage in which a borrower receives a below-market interest rate in return for which the lender (or another investor such as a family member or other partner) receives a portion of the future appreciation in the value of the property. May also apply to mortgage where the borrowers share the monthly principal and interest payments with another party in exchange for part of the appreciation.

Simple Interest
Interest which is computed only on the principal balance.

Survey
A measurement of land, prepared by a registered land surveyor, showing the location of the land with reference to know points, its dimensions, and the location and dimensions of any buildings.

Sweat Equity
Equity created by a purchaser performing work on a property being purchased.

Term Mortgage
See Balloon Payment Mortgage

Title
A document that gives evidence of an individual's ownership of property.

Title Insurance
A policy, usually issued by a title insurance company, which insures a home buyer against errors in the title search. The cost of the policy is usually a function of the value of the property, and is often borne by the purchaser and/or seller.

Title Search
An examination of municipal records to determine the legal ownership of property. Usually is performed by an attorney or title company.

Truth-In-Lending
A federal law requiring disclosure of the Annual Percentage Rate and other loan terms to home buyers within 72 hours of loan application per regulation.

Two-Step Mortgage
A mortgage in which the borrower receives a below-market interest rate for a specified number of years most often (7 or 10), and then receives a new interest rate adjusted (within certain limits) to market conditions at that time. The lender sometimes has the option to call the loan due within 30 days notice at the end of 7 or 10 years. Also called "Super Seven" or "Premier" mortgage.

Underwriting
The decision whether to make a loan to a potential home buyer based on income, assists, credit, collateral and other factors and the matching of this risk to an appropriate rate and term or loan amount.

USURY
Interest charged in excess of the legal rate established by law.

VA loan
A long-term, low-or no-down payment loan guaranteed by the Department of Veterans Affairs. Restricted to individuals qualified by military service or other entitlements.

VA Mortgage Funding Fee
A premium of up to 3% (depending of the size of the down payment, and previous use of benefits) paid on a VA-backed loan. An eligible veteran who is using his eligibility for the first time will pay a 2% funding fee which can be financed.

Variable Rate Mortgage (VRM)
see Adjustable Rate Mortgage.

Verification of Deposit (VOD)
A document signed by the borrower's financial institution verifying the status and balance of his/her financial accounts. This document is generally not needed if recent bank statements are available.

Verification of Employment (VOE)
A document signed by the borrower's employer verifying his/her position and salary. This document is generally not needed if recent pay stubs are available.

Warehouse Fee
Many mortgage firms must borrow funds on a short term basis in order to originate loans which are to be sold later in the secondary mortgage market (or to investors). When the prime rate of interest is higher on short term loans than on mortgage loans, the mortgage firm has an economic loss which is offset by charging a warehouse fee.

Onward we go, learning more how to be a highly paid professional mortgage loan officer!

Appendix

The forms in this section are some of the many forms used in the mortgage loan process. This is not meant to be a complete or comprehensive list and these forms are in an ever changing mode as the need arises from state or federal directives. These forms are meant as a guide only, and in no way represents legal advice concerning the validity or usage of the forms. They are used for us internally only. Many other forms are also used in connection with the lending process.

Computer Generated GFE
Truth In Lending Form
Prepaid Finance Charges
Borrowers Statement Regarding Military Activity
Borrowers Certification and Authorization
Notice To Applicants
Transfer Of Loan Servicing Disclosure
Notice of Right To Receive A Copy Of Your Appraisal-ECOA-B
Notice to Applicant-ECOA-A
Good Faith Estimate Attachment
Privacy Policy Notice
Additional Disclosure For Fixed Rate Loans
Mortgage Broker/Loan Officer Disclosure
Credit Score Notice
Settlement Worksheet
Stacking Order
Qualification Worksheet
Instructions To Clients
Conversation Log

GOOD FAITH ESTIMATE

Applicants:	**Benny Borrower**
Property Addr:	**1234 Main Street, Houston, TX 77060**
Prepared By:	**TEXAS SUPREME MORTGAGE INC. Ph. 281-445-1901**
	505 N. SAM HOUSTON PKWY. E. STE.110, HOUSTON, TX 77060

Application No:	**CONV**
Date Prepared:	**04/01/2005**
Loan Program:	**CONV**

The information provided below reflects estimates of the charges which you are likely to incur at the settlement of your loan. The fees listed are estimates-actual charges may be more or less. Your transaction may not involve a fee for every item listed. The numbers listed beside the estimates generally correspond to the numbered lines contained in the HUD-1 settlement statement which you will be receiving at settlement. The HUD-1 settlement statement will show you the actual cost for items paid at settlement.

Total Loan Amount $ **237,500**   Interest Rate: **5.500** %   Term: **360 / 360** mths

800	ITEMS PAYABLE IN CONNECTION WITH LOAN:			
801	Loan Origination Fee	1.000%	$	2,375.00	PFC
802	Loan Discount				PFC
803	Appraisal Fee		350.00	
804	Credit Report		75.00	
805	Lender's Inspection Fee			
808	Mortgage Broker Fee			
809	Tax Related Service Fee		150.00	PFC
810	Processing Fee		500.00	PFC
811	Underwriting Fee		150.00	PFC
812	Wire Transfer Fee			
	QUALITY CONTROL		150.00	PFC
	COURIER/FED EX		100.00	PFC

1100	TITLE CHARGES:			
1101	Closing or Escrow Fee:	$	100.00	PFC
1105	Document Preparation Fee		250.00	
1106	Notary Fees			
1107	Attorney Fees			
1108	Title Insurance:		175.00	

1200	GOVERNMENT RECORDING & TRANSFER CHARGES:		
1201	Recording Fees:	$	45.00
1202	City/County Tax/Stamps:		
1203	State Tax/Stamps:		

1300	ADDITIONAL SETTLEMENT CHARGES:		
1302	Pest Inspection	$	
	SURVEY		360.00

		Estimated Closing Costs	4,780.00

900	ITEMS REQUIRED BY LENDER TO BE PAID IN ADVANCE:				
901	Interest for	15 days @ $	36.2847	per day	$	544.27	PFC
902	Mortgage Insurance Premium			
903	Hazard Insurance Premium		1,800.00	
904				
905	VA Funding Fee			

144

1000	RESERVES DEPOSITED WITH LENDER:						
1001	Hazard Insurance Premiums	3	months @ $	150.00	per month	$	450.00
1002	Mortgage Ins. Premium Reserves	2	months @ $	175.00	per month		350.00
1003	School Tax		months @ $		per month		
1004	Taxes and Assessment Reserves	3	months @ $	500.00	per month		1,500.00
1005	Flood Insurance Reserves		months @ $		per month		
			months @ $		per month		
			months @ $		per month		

		Estimated Prepaid Items/Reserves	4,644.27
TOTAL ESTIMATED SETTLEMENT CHARGES			9,424.27

COMPENSATION TO BROKER (Not Paid Out of Loan Proceeds):		
Yield Spread Premium 0-4%	$	

TOTAL ESTIMATED FUNDS NEEDED TO CLOSE:				TOTAL ESTIMATED MONTHLY PAYMENT:	
Purchase Price/Payoff (+)	250,000.00	New First Mortgage(-)		Principal & Interest	1,348.50
Loan Amount (-)	237,500.00	Sub Financing(-)		Other Financing (P & I)	
Est. Closing Costs (+)	4,780.00	New 2nd Mtg Closing Costs(+)		Hazard Insurance	150.00
Est. Prepaid Items/Reserves (+)	4,644.27			Real Estate Taxes	500.00
Amount Paid by Seller (-)				Mortgage Insurance	175.00
				Homeowner Assn. Dues	
				Other	
Total Est. Funds needed to close			21,924.27	Total Monthly Payment	2,173.50

☑ This Good Faith Estimate is being provided by **TEXAS SUPREME MORTGAGE INC.**   , a mortgage broker, and no lender has been obtained. **These estimates are provided pursuant to the Real Estate Settlement Procedures Act of 1974, as amended (RESPA). Additional information can be found in the HUD Special Information Booklet, which is to be provided to you by your mortgage broker or lender, if your application is to purchase residential real property and the lender will take a first lien on the property.** The undersigned acknowledges receipt of the booklet "Settlement Costs," and if applicable the Consumer Handbook on ARM Mortgages.

Applicant **Benny Borrower** _____ Date _____   Applicant _____ Date _____

TRUTH-IN-LENDING DISCLOSURE STATEMENT
(THIS IS NEITHER A CONTRACT NOR A COMMITMENT TO LEND)

Applicants:	**Benny Borrower**	Prepared By:	**TEXAS SUPREME MORTGAGE INC.** **505 N. SAM HOUSTON PKWY. E. STE.110**
Property Address:	**1234 Main Street** **Houston, TX 77060**		**HOUSTON , TX 77060** **281-445-1901**
Application No:	**CONV**	Date Prepared:	**04/01/2005**

ANNUAL PERCENTAGE RATE	FINANCE CHARGE	AMOUNT FINANCED	TOTAL OF PAYMENTS
The cost of your credit as a yearly rate	The dollar amount the credit will cost you	The amount of credit provided to you or on your behalf	The amount you will have paid after making all payments as scheduled
* 6.285 %	$ * 273,553.36	$ * 233,430.73	$ * 506,984.09

☐ REQUIRED DEPOSIT: The annual percentage rate does not take into account your required deposit
PAYMENTS: Your payment schedule will be:

Number of Payments	Amount of Payments **	When Payments Are Due	Number of Payments	Amount of Payments **	When Payments Are Due	Number of Payments	Amount of Payments **	When Payments Are Due
		Monthly Beginning:			Monthly Beginning:			Monthly Beginning:
123	1,523.50	06/01/2005						
236	1,348.50	09/01/2015						
1	1,347.59	05/01/2035						

☐ DEMAND FEATURE: This obligation has a demand feature.
☐ VARIABLE RATE FEATURE: This loan contains a variable rate feature. A variable rate disclosure has been provided earlier.

CREDIT LIFE/CREDIT DISABILITY: Credit life insurance and credit disability insurance are not required to obtain credit, and will not be provided unless you sign and agree to pay the additional cost.

Type	Premium	Signature	
Credit Life		I want credit life insurance.	Signature:
Credit Disability		I want credit disability insurance.	Signature:
Credit Life and Disability		I want credit life and disability insurance.	Signature:

INSURANCE: The following insurance is required to obtain credit: **HAZARD INSURANCE**

☐ Credit life insurance ☐ Credit disability ☐ Property insurance ☐ Flood insurance

You may obtain the insurance from anyone you want that is acceptable to creditor

☐ If you purchase ☑ property ☐ flood insurance from creditor you will pay $ _____ for a one year term.

SECURITY: You are giving a security interest in:

☐ The goods or property being purchased ☐ Real property you already own.

FILING FEES: $ **45.00**

LATE CHARGE: If a payment is more than **15** days late, you will be charged **5.000** % of the payment

PREPAYMENT: If you pay off early, you

☐ may ☑ will not have to pay a penalty.

☐ may ☑ will not be entitled to a refund of part of the finance charge.

ASSUMPTION: Someone buying your property

☐ may ☐ may, subject to conditions ☑ may not assume the remainder of your loan on the original terms.

See your contract documents for any additional information about nonpayment, default, any required repayment in full before the scheduled date and prepayment refunds and penalties

☑ * means an estimate ☑ all dates and numerical disclosures except the late payment disclosures are estimates.

* * NOTE: The Payments shown above include reserve deposits for Mortgage Insurance (if applicable), but exclude Property Taxes and Insurance.

THE UNDERSIGNED ACKNOWLEDGES RECEIVING A COMPLETED COPY OF THIS DISCLOSURE.

Benny Borrower	(Applicant) (Date)	(Applicant) (Date)
	(Applicant) (Date)	(Applicant) (Date)
	(Lender) (Date)	

Calyx Form - til.hp (02/95)

Prepaid Finance Charges

The following items are to be used in determining PFC amounts on the Truth In Lending to calculate Annual percentage Rate (APR):

FEE	PFC/NOT PFC	FEE	PFC/NOT PFC
Administrative	PFC	Ammo Schedule	PFC
Application	PFC	Appraisal	Not PFC
Appraisal Review	PFC	Assignment	PFC
Assumption	PFC	Attorney-Inside	PFC
Attorney-Outside	Not PFC	Mortgage Broker	PFC
Borrower Buydown	PFC	Closing (to lender)	PFC
Closing (to Title Co)	PFC	Commitment	PFC
Compliance	PFC	Courier	PFC
Credit Report	Not PFC	Delivery	PFC
Discount	PFC	Doc Prep-outside Attny	Not PFC
Doc Prep-			
By other than outside Attny	PFC	Document Review	PFC
Engineer	Not PFC	Escrow Waiver	PFC
FHA Funding	PFC	Filing	Not PFC
Flood Determination	Not PFC	Funding	PFC
Guaranty	PFC	Hazard Insurance	Not PFC
Inspection-general	Not PFC	Inspection-	
		New construction	PFC
Prepaid Interest	PFC	Lock	PFC
Mortgage Insurance (MI)	PFC	MI Reserves	PFC
Notary	Not PFC	Origination	PFC
Overnight Mail	PFC	Pest Inspection	Not PFC
Points Paid By Seller	Not PFC	Processing	PFC
Recording	Not PFC	Refinance	PFC
Reserves For Non-PFC	Not PFC	Reserves For PFC Items	PFC
Survey	Not PFC	Tax Service	PFC
Title Insurance	Not PFC	Title Policy	Not PFC
Transfer	PFC	Underwriting	PFC
VA Funding	PFC	Warehouse	PFC
Wire	PFC		

DISCLAIMER: This list is in no way comprehensive, and several items are subject to interpretation. If you can figure this out any better than described here, please notify your congressman and be a hero to the industry for simplifying this procedure!

Borrower(S) Statement Regarding Active Duty Military

I am a member of a Military Reserve or National Guard unit.

Borrower: Co-Borrower:

_____ Yes   _____ Yes

_____ No   _____ No

I have been notified and/or received orders for mobilization of military or National Guard unit.

Borrower: Co-Borrower:

_____ Yes   _____ Yes

_____ No   _____ No

_____   _____
Borrower's Signature   Date

_____   _____
Co-Borrower's Signature   Date

LENDER: TEXAS SUPREME MORTGAGE, INC.

BORROWER:

PROPERTY ADDRESS:
LOAN NO.:

BORROWERS(S) CERTIFICATION & AUTHORIZATION

I/we have applied for a mortgage loan from the Lender shown hereon. The application I/we completed contains various information about the purpose of the loan, the amount and source of the down payment, employment and income information, assets and liabilities. I/we certify that the information supplied is true and complete. I/we have made no misrepresentations in the loan application or other documents, nor did I/we omit any pertinent information. I/we agree to inform the lender in the event that there is a significant change in my/our employment or financial status prior to the settlement date.

I/we fully understand that it is a federal crime, punishable by fine or imprisonment, or both, to knowingly make false statements when applying for this mortgage, as applicable under the provisions of Title 18, United States Code, Section 101.

BY SIGNING BELOW, I/we authorize Lender, its successors or assigns and the mortgage guaranty insurer (if any), to acquire any credit reports, credit history and verification of any items, prior or current, to aid in the approval, processing or closing of my/our mortgage loan or as part of the lenders quality control program. Permission is hereby granted to Lender to verify, existing or prior accounts, for example, but not limited to the following: First or second mortgage loan accounts, land contracts, rentals, credit union or other installment loans, credit card accounts, money market accounts, savings accounts, employment income/history, tax returns and any account required for deposit, down payment or collateral for the mortgage loan. I/we understand that the confidentiality of the acquired information will be preserved except where disclosure of the information is required by applicable law and that the information will be transmitted directly form the verifying source to the Lender and will not be transmitted through myself/ourselves or any other party.

I/we ☐ **plan to** ☐ **do not plan to use** the acquired property as our ☐ principal residence ☐ secondary residence.

TO WHOM IT MAY CONCERN: My/our signature(s) here authorize(s) you to furnish the information requested by the above named Lender or Lender's agent without additional signatures on forms for verifying the items listed above. These requests for verification are to be accepted as if my/our signature(s) were present on the form(s). My/our name typed or printed in the authorized signature area on the verification form(s) along with a copy of this authorization can be accepted as permission to supply this information. A copy of this form may be accepted as an original.

Privacy Act Notice Statement – This information is to be used by the agency collecting it in determining whether you qualify as a prospective mortgagor for mortgage insurance or guaranty or as a borrower for a rehabilitation loan under the agency's program. It will not be disclosed outside the agency without your consent except to financial institutions for verification of your deposits and as required and permitted by law. You do not have to give us this information, but, if you do not, your application for approval as a prospective mortgagor for mortgage insurance or guaranty or as a borrower for a rehabilitation loan my be delayed or rejected. This information requested is authorized by Title 38, U.S.C., Chapter 37 (if VA); by 12 U.S.C., Section 1701 et seq., (if HUD/FHA); and by 42 U.S.C., Section 1452b (if HUD/CPD).

COMPLIANCE AGREEMENT

Should this mortgage loan be approved, Borrower(s) agree, if requested by the Lender, its successors and/or assigns, the closing agent for the Lender or the mortgage guaranty insurer (if any), to fully cooperate in the adjustment or correction of any errors including those of a clerical nature on any or all loan documentation.

Borrower(s) also agree to cooperate with Lender in supplying or correcting any documentation deemed necessary by the Lender, its successors or assigns and/or the mortgage guaranty insurer (if any), for the purpose of the transfer, sale or conveyance by Lender of its interest in and to said loan documentation to any entity, including, but not limited to, any investor, the Federal National Mortgage Association, the Federal Home Loan Mortgage Corporation, the Federal Housing Administration or the Veterans Administration.

_____   _____ Date:_____

Borrower Signature   Social Security No.

_____   _____ Date:_____

Co-Borrower Signature   Social Security No.

NOTICE TO APPLICANTS

Under the Federal Income Tax Law, you are subject to certain penalties if you do not provide us with your correct Social Security number or other taxpayer identification number. Please read this notice carefully.

The tax reform act of 1984 requires lenders to report interest received from an individual on a loan secured by real estate if the total interest received on the loan during the years is $600.00 or more. The interest received and the borrower's taxpayer identification number must be reported to the Internal Revenue Service. This will allow the Internal Revenue Service to verify deduction for interest paid on loans secured by real estate.

You (as a borrower) are required to provide your taxpayer identification number to us (as a lender). If you are an individual, your taxpayer identification number is your Social Security number. You may be subject to a $50.00 penalty imposed by the Internal Revenue Service if you do not provide us with your correct taxpayer identification number.

Please supply your taxpayer identification number and the other information requested on the form on the bottom of this notice.

_____

Borrower's Name:_____   Co-Borrower's Name:_____

Address:_____   Address:_____

_____   _____

Taxpayer I.D. #:_____   Taxpayer I.D. #:_____

Signature:_____   Signature:_____

I am an individual?   Yes   No   I am an
individual?   Yes   No

_____
notice.wps

TRANSFER OF LOAN SERVICING DISCLOSURE

BORROWER(S): _____

PROPERTY: _____

In compliance with the National Affordable Housing Act, you are hereby notified that Texas National Mortgage, Inc. may elect to assign, sell or transfer the servicing of your loan to another mortgage servicer at any time while your loan is still outstanding. If this option is exercised by Texas National Mortgage, Inc., you will be notified with the proper notice.

Texas Supreme Mortgage, Inc. does not have the capacity to service your loan, and will assign, sell or transfer your loan to another servicer. Texas National Mortgage, Inc. presently intends to assign, sell or transfer approximately 100% of loan servicing during the next 12 months. This percentage is the best estimate available at this time.

Servicing procedures, transfer practices & requirements and complaint resolution will be in accordance with the model disclosure statement developed by the Department Of Housing and Urban Development ("HUD").

I/WE have read and understand this transfer of servicing disclosure.

_____ _____   _____ _____
Borrower   Date   Co-Borrower   Date

transfr1.wps

Notice Of Right To Receive A Copy Of Your Appraisal
ECOA-B

You have the right to a copy of the appraisal report, if any, used in connection with your application for credit.   If you wish to receive a copy, please write to us at the mailing address below.   Please type or print, sign and date your request, and include the following information for your request home mortgage loan or consumer loan appraisal report:

FULL NAME:_____

MAILING ADDRESS:_____

                _____

TELEPHONE NUMBER:_____

We must be contacted within ninety (90) days of notification of action on your loan application to process this request.

I/WE acknowledge receipt of this notice.

_____   _____
Borrower   Co-Borrower

_____
Date

                 TEXAS SUPREME MORTGAGE, INC.
                 505 N. SAM HOUSTON PKWY., E., #110
                 HOUSTON, TEXAS 77060

_____
ecoa-b.wps

NOTICE TO APPLICANTS

In accordance with provisions of the Federal Equal Credit Opportunity Act (15 U.S.C. 1691 etseg.) effective March 23, 1977, the following information is provided for your loan guidance prior to your application to Texas Supreme Mortgage, Inc., for a Real Estate loan:

1. The Federal Equal Credit Opportunity Act prohibits creditors from discrimination against credit applicants on basis of race, color, religion, national origin, sex, marital status, age (provided the applicant has the capacity to enter into a binding contract): because all or part of the applicant's income derives from any public assistance program: Or because the applicant has in good faith exercised any right under the consumer credit protection act. The Federal Agency that administers compliance with this law concerning the mortgage loan company is the:

> Federal Trade Commission
> Equal Credit Opportunity
> Washington, D.C. 20580

2. You need not disclose income from alimony, child support or separate maintenance unless you desire such income to be considered in determining credit worthiness.

3. You may be asked to answer questions regarding your race, national origin, sex, marital status, and age. You do not have to answer such questions if you do not wish to do so, but we are required to ask them for the reason that such information is being requested by the Federal Government to monitor compliance with Federal Anti-Discrimination status, which status prohibits creditors from discrimination against applicants on those bases.

4. If a courtesy title is included in the Application (such as Mr., Mrs., Ms., Miss), providing such information is optional.

5. You are entitled to a notice by this office of action taken on your application within 30 days of our receipt of all exhibits and matters necessary to complete your application. If adverse action is taken on your application, said notice shall contain a statement of specific reason for action taken.

I (we) the undersigned, acknowledge that I (we) have read and understand foregoing

Borrower   Date

Co-Borrower   Date

_____

notapp2.wps

155

GOOD FAITH ESTIMATE ATTACHMENT

The following information is being furnished by the lender because of a particular provider of service or may be required. The estimates set forth on the Good Faith Estimate are based on charges by the provider. Where particular providers are named below, the lender has used or required the use of such providers in the last twelve months.

APPRAISERS

Ed Woodruff & Assoc.
4420 F.M., 1960 W., #220
Houston, TX 77068
281-440-4881

Bowden Appraisal Group
321 Sawdust Road
Spring, TX 77380
281-367-4248

CREDIT REPORTING AGENCIES

Factual Data
15311 Vantage Parkway West, Ste., 320
Houston, TX 77032
281-442-1313

DP Credit Service, Inc.
9513 Burnet Road, Ste 204
Austin, TX 78758
1-800-319-6060

SURVEYORS

Bowden Surveying, Inc.
P.O. Box 441692
Houston, TX 77244
281-531-1900

Horne Land Services, LLP
1733 Woodstead Ct., #110
The Woodlands, TX 77380
281-296-2550

PROCESSING

Elite Processing Center
505 N. Sam Houston Pkwy.,E., Suite 110
Houston, TX 77060
281-447-3195

CityWide Processing
440 Benmar Dr., Ste 1065
Houston, TX 77060
281-445-1333

_____   _____
Borrower   Date   Co-Borrower   Date

PRIVACY POLICY NOTICE

This notice is provided to you pursuant to the Privacy of Consumer Financial Information Act and the Federal Trade Commission's implementing regulation there-under, 16 CFR Part 313.

1.   Collection Sources:

        We collect nonpublic personal information about you from the following sources:

        -       Information we receive from you on applications or other forms;
        -       Information about you transactions with us, our affiliates, or others;
                And
        -       Information we receive from a consumer reporting agency.

2.   We do not disclose any nonpublic personal information about our customers or former customers to anyone, except as permitted by law.

3.   We restrict access to nonpublic personal information about your to those employees who need to know that information to provide the requested loan origination services to you. We maintain physical, electronic, and procedural safeguards that comply with federal regulations to guard your nonpublic personal information.

By signing below, you acknowledge receipt of this Notice.

_____
Borrower   (date)

_____
Co-Borrower   (date)

ADDITIONAL DISCLOSURE FOR FIXED RATE LOANS

You have received an application for a fixed rate loan. The following is a description of the key terms of fixed rate loans offered by Texas Supreme Mortgage, Inc. (TSMI) to qualified applicants. TSMI may and will be used interchangeably with "lender".

Key Terms:
Loan Amount: $_____   Term of Maturity: ____ Months

INTEREST RATE: The interest rate, if known will be _____% otherwise, the interest rate on your loan will be disclosed to you on the loan closing date and will be based on market conditions at the time and your acceptance of loan conditions.

INITIAL PRINCIPAL AND INTEREST PAYMENT AMOUNT: The initial principal and interest payment amount depends on the interest rate and term. The amount of payment ( ) is not known at this time or ( ) will be $_____ monthly or ( ) is estimated to be $_____ monthly based on the interest rate listed above.

AMORTIZATION: the amortization period for your loan is __TBD__ months. The monthly payments on your loan have been estimated so as to repay all principal and interest by the end of the amortization period.

DEFAULT AND FORECLOSURE OF YOUR LOAN: Your loan will be in default if any of the following events occur:
1. You fail to make any monthly payments on time or fail to pay the final installment of you loan at maturity.
2. You fail to make any escrow payments for taxes and insurance or, if no escrow payments are required by TSMI, you fail to keep the property insured or fail to pay the taxes as required by the deed of trust.
3. You fail to maintain the property or fail to perform any obligations or pay any assessment required by your homeowners association, if applicable.
4. You become insolvent or bankrupt, or the property is condemned by eminent domain.
5. You sell or convey the property or any interest without TSMI prior written consent.
6. Your loan is made unenforceable by legislation or law.

In event of a default on your loan, TSMI may at its option declare your loan immediately due and payable in full. If all sums then owed to TSMI are not paid by you upon receipt of the demands by TSMI, TSMI will then institute action to sell your property at a foreclosure sale pursuant to the terms of the Deed of Trust you will execute at closing.

FEES: You will be charged fees by TSMI and other persons in connections with the origination of your loan. TSMI will give you an estimate of these fees within three business days after receiving your loan application, or at loan application.

Broker: TSMI is a loan broker. The broker is not acting as your agent and in no way is making any guarantees as to the approval or success of your loan application. TSMI is and Independent Contractor for the purpose of seeking your financing. You have also executed as a separate agreement, the Mortgage Loan Origination Agreement. The broker will receive compensation for services rendered direct from the lender.

Please acknowledge that you have read and received this disclosure by signing below.

_____   _____
Applicant   Co-Applicant

_____   _____
Date   Date

MORTGAGE BROKER/LOAN OFFICER DISCLOSURE

Mortgage Broker or Loan Officer: _____

License Number: _____

This information in this disclosure is provided to clarify the nature of our relationship, my duties to you, and how I am to be compensated as a mortgage Broker or Loan Office. This disclosure is a requirement of the TMBLA.

Since I may be working for a company, references to "we" or "us" refer to me and any company for which I am working.

Duties and Nature of Relationship (Check ALL that apply)
You, the applicant(s), have applied with us for a residential mortgage loan.

(x)   We will submit your loan application to a participating lender which we may from time to time contract upon such terms as you may request or a lender may require. In connection with this mortgage loan, we are acting as an independent contractor and not as your agent. We will enter into separate independent contractor agreements with various lenders. While we will seek to assist you in meeting your financial needs, we do not distribute the products of all lenders or investors in the market and cannot guarantee the lowest or best terms available in the market.

( )   In connection with this mortgage loan, we are acting as an independent contractor and not as your agent. We will make your loan ourselves. We may either sell the loan to an investor or retain it. (You will receive a separate disclosure as to how we will handle servicing rights on any such loan.) We have a number of established independent contractor relationships with various investors to whom we sell closed loans. We are not an agent for any such investor in connection with the sale of the loan. While we seek to assist you in meeting your financial needs, we cannot guarantee the lowest or best terms available in the market.

( )   We will be acting as follows:

How we will be compensated:

(x)   The retail price we offer you, your interest rate, total points, and fees, will include our compensation. In some cases we may be paid all or part of our compensation by you or by the lender or investor. Alternatively, we may be paid a portion of our compensation by both you and the lender. For example, in some cases, if you would rather pay a lower interest rate, you may pay higher up-front points and fees. Also, in some cases, if you would rather pay less up-front, you may be able to pay a higher rate, in which case some or all of my compensation will be paid by the lender. We also may be paid by the lender based on other goods, services, or facilities performed or provided by us to the lender.

( )   Our pricing for you loan is based upon current wholesale options available to us in the secondary market where closed loans are sold. Fees charged directly to you by us may vary depending on the type of loan for which you have applied.

At the time of this disclosure, we are receiving $_____ in fees:
The services for which these fees are being charged include the following:
( ) Application Fee $_____
( ) Processing Fee $_____
( ) Appraisal Fee $_____

( ) Credit Report Fee $_____

( ) Automated underwriting Fee $_____

Other (list)

      _____ $_____

      _____ $_____

Of this amount, $_____is **not refundable** under any conditions.

The remainder of this amount will not be subject to refund at any time after we have ordered or obtained the services for which such fees are being collected.

The estimated fees which we will charge will be as shown on the good faith estimate which we are providing to you now or which we will provide you within three (3) days in accordance with the requirements of the Real Estate Settlement Procedures Act and its implementing regulations.

10A

P2 MORTGAGE BROKER/LOAN OFFICER DISCLOSURE

Texas Supreme Mortgage, Inc., IS LICENSED UNDER THE LAWS OF THE STATE OF TEXAS AND BY STATE LAW IS SUBJECT TO REGULATORY OVERSIGHT BY THE TEXAS SAVINGS AND LOAN DEPARTMENT. ANY CONSUMER WISHING TO FILE A COMPLAINT AGAINST **Texas Supreme Mortgage, Inc.,** SHOULD COMPLETE, SIGN, AND SEND A COMPLAINT FORM TO THE TEXAS SAVINGS AND LOAN DEPARTMENT AT 2601 NORTH LAMAR, SUITE 201, AUSTIN, TEXAS 78705. COMPAINT FORMS AND INSTRUCTIONS MAY BE DOWNLOADED AND PRINTED FROM THE DEPARTMENTS WEB SITE LOCATED AT **WWW.TSLS.ST.TX.US**, OR OBTAINED FROM THE DEPARTMENT UPON REQUEST BY MAIL AT THE ADDRESS ABOVE, BY TELEPHONE AT IT'S TOLL-FREE CONSUMER HOTLINE AT 1-877-276-5550, BY FAX AT (512) 475-1360, OR BY E-MAIL AT **TSLD@TSLD.STATE.TX.US**

THE DEPARTMENT MAINTAINS THE MORTGAGE BROKER RECOVERY FUND TO MAKE PAYMENTS OF CERTAIN TYPES OF JUDGMENTS AGAINST A MORTGAGE BROKER OR LOAN OFFICER. NOT ALL CLAIMS ARE COMPENSABLE AND COURT MUST ORDER THE PAYMENT OF A CLAIM FROM THE RECOVERY FUND BEFORE THE DEPARTMENT MAY PAY A CLAIM. FOR MORE INFORMATION ABOUT THE RECOVERY FUND, PLEASE CONSULT SUBCHAPTER F OF THE MORTGAGE BROKER LICENSE ACT OF THE DEPARTMENTS WEBSITE REFERENCED ABOVE.

Applicant(s):   Mortgage Broker/Loan Officer:

Signed:_____   Signed:_____

Signed:_____

Name:_____   Name:

Date:_____   Date:_____

CREDIT SCORE NOTICE	
BORROWER NAME(S):	LENDER: _TEXAS_ _SUPREME MORTGAGE, INC._ 505 N. SAM HOUSTON PKWY E. STE 110 HOUSTON, TX 77060 281-445-1901 DATE:

NOTICE TO THE HOME LOAN APPLICANT

In connection with your application for a home loan, the lender must disclose to you the score that a consumer reporting agency distributed to users and the lender used in connection with your home loan, and the key factors affecting your credit scores.

The credit score is a computer generated summary calculated at the time of the request and based on information that a consumer reporting agency or lender has on file. The scores are based on data about your credit history and payment patterns. Credit scores are important because they are used to assist the lender in determining whether you will obtain a loan. They may also be used to determine what interest rate you may be offered on the mortgage. Credit scores can change over time, depending on your conduct, how your credit history and payment patterns change, and how credit scoring technologies change.

Because the score is based on information in your credit history, it is very important that you review the credit-related information that is being furnished to make sure it is accurate. Credit records may vary from one company to another.

If you have questions about your credit score or the credit information that is furnished to you, contact the consumer reporting agency at the address and telephone number provided with this notice, or contact the lender. If the lender developed or generated the credit score. The consumer reporting agency plays no part in the decision to take any action on the loan application and is unable to provide you with specific reasons for the decision on a loan application.

If you have questions concerning the terms of the loan, contact the lender.

One or more of the following consumer reporting agencies will provide the credit score:

Experian
P.O. Box 2002
Allen, TX 75013
1-888-397-3742

Equifax Credit Information Services
P.O. Box 740241
Atlanta, GA 30374
1-800-685-1111

Trans Union
P.O. Box 4000
Chester, PA 19016
1-888-887-2673

Your acknowledgment below signifies that this written notice was provided to you.

_____	_____	_____	_____
Borrower	Date	Borrower	Date
_____	_____	_____	_____
Borrower	Date	Borrower	Date
_____	_____	_____	_____
Borrower	Date	Borrower	Date
_____	_____	_____	_____
Borrower	Date	Borrower	Date

Settlement Closeout Worksheet

Application Date:_____   Investor:_____

TSMI LOAN #:_____   Investor Loan #:_____
　　　　　(Home Office to assign)

Loan Officer_____   Investor Phone #_____

File Name: Borrower_____   Ofc Phone:_____

　　　Co-Borrower:_____   Ofc. Phone:_____

Property Address:_____ _____ _____
　　　　　　　　　　　(Street Address)　　　　　　　　　　　　(City)　　　　　(Zip)

Current Home Phone #:_____

Selling Broker & Agent:_____ _____ _____
　　　　　　　　　　(Agency)　　　　　　　(Agent)　　　　　(Ofc. Phone)

Listing Broker & Agent:_____ _____ _____
　　　　　　　　　　(Agency)　　　　　　　(Agent)　　　　　(Ofc. Phone)

Sales Price: $_____   Mortgage Amount: $_____

LTV:_____%; Closed Rate:_____%:   Fixed Rate/ARM;   Term:_____ Years;

Single Family, Condo, Townhouse, Multi Family/Land   Purchase_____
　　　　　(circle one)

Owner Occupied/Investor:_____   Refi: R&T_____ C/O _____

Origination:_____% Discount/Broker Fee:_____% Premium:_____%
Date:
Submitted:_____   Closed:_____   Funded:_____

Settlement

Originaton Fee:　　　　　　_____% $_____

Premium: From Investor   _____% $_____

Broker Fee Charged:　　　_____% $_____

Net Premium & Broker Fee:　　　　　　$_____

Ancillary Fees Collected At Closing　　　　$_____

```
┌─────────────────────────────────────────────────────────────────────────┐
│ Total Fees to Distribute: (Matches Title Company Check)      $_____  │
│                                                                           │
│ Home Office To Complete This Section!                                     │
│                                                                           │
│ Originator $_____    TSMI Fees: Closing:        $ _____     │
│                                                                           │
│                               TSMI Monthly Min:            _____     │
│                                                                           │
│                               ($100 X Number Of Months Since Last Closing)│
│                                                                           │
│                                   TSMI Other Fees:      _____        │
│                                                                           │
│                                   Total TSMI Fees:$     _____        │
│                                                                           │
│                                                                           │
│                                                                           │
└─────────────────────────────────────────────────────────────────────────┘
```

(LO 100% Settlement Worksheet)

STACKING ORDER

NOTE: *Loan Officer/Processor must complete and sign this stacking order before checks are released to the Loan Officer.* **Make sure that each form is completed as to borrower, property address, any additional information requested, signed by all parties, and dated consistently with the application date.**

_____

____

Right Side   **PROCEDURE**

____   1)   Settlement Worksheet
____   2).   Certified HUD & Check Copy   1) Check all that apply.
____   3).   Final 1008 & Final 1003   2) Put N/A by any items that
____   4).   Underwriting Findings From Lender   Do Not Apply to this loan.
____   5).   Initial 1003-Borrower Signed   3) Fasten all paperwork
____   6).   All Credit Reports   on each side, and tape over
____   7).   Verifications (VOM, VOE, VOD, VOR)   back of fastener.
____   8).   Pay stubs and bank statements   4) Turn in with all monies
____   9).   Signed Earnest Money Contract (if applicable)   from title company.
____   10). Title Commitment & Tax Certificates.   5) Include latest copy of all
____   11). Survey   source documents only.
____   12). Appraisal
____   13). Home Owners Insurance
____   14). Copy Of Drivers license, SS card or ID card.

Left Side:
____   15). Disclosures
              ____   Stacking Order
              ____   Conversation Log
              ____   Credit Score Notice
              ____   GFE (initial) (Evidence of Delivery Within 3 Days Of Application
              ____   TIL (initial) (Evidence of Delivery Within 3 Days Of Application,
                      Follow PFC List, APR MUST be greater than Note Rate)
              ____   Mortgage Broker/Loan Officer Disclosure (As Promulgated by State
                      Statutes)
              ____   Additional Disclosure For Fixed Rate Loans (If Applicable)
              ____   Borrowers Statement Concerning Military Duty
              ____   Borrower Certification/ Authorization
              ____   Notice To Applicants -- Notice concerning SS#'s
              ____   Transfer Of Loan Servicing Disclosure Statement
              ____   Notice Of Right To Receive Appraisal (ECOA-B)
              ____   Notice to Applicants (ECOA) (Non-Discrimination Notice)
              ____   GFE Attachment (Service Provider Disclosure)
              ____   Privacy Policy Notice
              ____   Rate Lock Confirmation
              ____   12 Day Letter on Cash Out Refi's (If required)

_____   Adjustable Rate Mtg. Disclosure (If required)
_____   Disclosure of Multiple Roles (If required)
_____   VA Disclosures   (If Required)
_____   Misc: Gift Letter, Use of Funds, Etc.
_____   17) All additional information and correspondence you feel may be helpful to TSLD.

NOTE: By signing this form you are certifying that all items listed are complete, true and correct.

Loan Officer: _____

Date: _____

You may have additional items in your file that are not relevant to the home office file.. I Highly suggest that you keep a copy package for your records. Home Office files are kept for three years after closing and will be destroyed in January of the following year.

(Lo 100% Stacking Order)

QUALIFICATION WORKSHEET

INCOME	NEW HOUSING PAYMENT

INCOME

Gross Monthly Income-Borr. $_____

              -Co-Borr _____

Child Support-Documented   _____

Real Estate Income-NET   _____

Other Documented Income   _____

TOTAL INCOME $_____
               (X)

ACTUAL RATIOS

HOUSING PMNT/INCOME = _____%
  (A) / (X)

TOTAL OBLIGATION/INCOME = _____%
  (C) / (X)

CALL:
Wes Cordeau
281-445-1901   T

NEW HOUSING PAYMENT

P & I $_____

Prop Taxes   _____

Hazard Ins   _____

HOA   _____

    Mtg Ins   _____

Other   _____

TOTAL PMNT $_____
            (A)

LIABILITIES (Monthly Payment)

Revolving $_____

Installment   _____

Auto 1   _____

Auto 2   _____

Child Support   _____

Other   _____

Total LIAB $_____
            (B)

TOTAL OBLIGATIONS: (A) + (B) = $_____
                   (C)

STATED RATIO MATRIX

	CONV	CONV 97	CHB	GOLD	JUMBO	VA	FHA	"B".
HOUSING	28	28	33	40	33	--	29	40.
OBLIGATIONS	38	36	38	40	38	41	41	50.

INSTRUCTIONS TO CLIENTS

During the course of this loan many items will come to you by mail or by phone: Examples are:

1. Truth In Lending - sign form and return to processor

2. Credit Report - review for accuracy & respond to any derogatory items in writing.   Explain and document these items.   Some one from the credit agency may call you directly.

3. An appraiser may call to set an appointment to inspect your home, only if you currently live in the home you are purchasing or refinancing.

4. As we progress through the loan, additional paycheck stubs, bank statements or other information may be required. Please keep your processor and/or loan officer current on these items.

5. During the first two weeks of loan processing, contact your insurance agent to issue a   quote for home insurance. **Have them fax us a copy.**

6. Once approved the underwriter may have additional questions. They will need to be addressed at once.

7. Once approved a termite inspection may be required. (Only on a purchase)

8. A cashier's check payable to the title company will be required at closing.

9. Please spell the Title Companies name exactly as it appears on your title commitment. **Also bring a picture ID to closing.**

A home loan requires **patience** and **persistence** to complete properly and timely.
We appreciate both and promise to complete your transaction in a timely and professional manner.

FINALLY: We promise to serve you faithfully, and expect you to **refer** at least two friends, relatives or co-workers to us during this transaction.   Please be on the lookout for these referrals. **THANKS**

Very Important Note: Please do not make any financial changes without informing your loan officer or processor BEFORE making any changes. Example's would be increasing, paying off or transferring any debts, changing employment, or switching banks. Finally, be sure to continue paying all monthly expenses in a timely manner.

Conversation Log

Date　　　**Who**　　　　　　　**Comments**

_____

_____

_____

_____

_____

_____

_____

_____

_____

_____

_____

_____

_____

_____

_____

_____

_____

Printed in the United States
121751LV00001B/177/A